Watching Hannah

PICTURING HISTORY

Series Editors
Peter Burke, Sander L. Gilman, Ludmilla Jordanova,
Roy Porter, †Bob Scribner (1995–8)

In the same series

Watching Hannah

Sexuality, Horror and Bodily De-formation in Victorian England

Barry Reay

REAKTION BOOKS

Published by Reaktion Books Ltd
79 Farringdon Road, London EC1M 3JU, UK

www.reaktionbooks.co.uk

First published 2002

Series design by Humphrey Stone
Printed and bound in Great Britain by
Bookcraft, Midsomer Norton

British Library Cataloguing in Publication Data

Reay, Barry, 1950–
    Watching Hannah: sexuality, horror and bodily de-formation
    in Victorian England. – (Picturing history)
    1. Munby, Arthur J. (Arthur Joseph), 1828–1910 – Views on
    working women 2. Women – Employment – Great Britain –
    History – 19th century
    I. Title
    305.4'2'0941'09034

ISBN 1 86189 119 9

Contents

Preface

The crowd is his domain, just as the air is the bird's, and water that of the fish. His passion and his profession is to merge with the crowd. For the perfect idler, for the passionate observer it becomes an immense source of enjoyment to establish his dwelling in the throng, in the ebb and flow, the bustle, the fleeting and the infinite. To be away from home and yet to feel at home anywhere; to see the world, to be at the very centre of the world, and yet to be unseen of the world, such are some of the minor pleasures of those independent, intense and impartial spirits, who do not lend themselves easily to linguistic definitions. The observer is a prince enjoying his incognito wherever he goes. The lover of life makes the whole world into his family, just as the lover of the fair sex creates his from all the lovely women he has found, from those that could be found, and those who are impossible to find, just as the picture-lover lives in an enchanted world of dreams painted on canvas. Thus the lover of universal life moves into the crowd as though into an enormous reservoir of electricity. He, the lover of life, may also be compared to a mirror as vast as this crowd; to a kaleidoscope endowed with consciousness, which with every one of its movements presents a pattern of life, in all its multiplicity, and the flowing grace of all the elements that go to compose life.[1]

Let us begin with a simple but dramatic representation: an eye, an eye being cut, like the famously disturbing image in Salvador Dalí and Luis Buñuel's film *Un Chien andalou* (1928), of the razor passing over the iris. But in this case, the eye is that of a poet and civil servant, one Arthur Munby, a connoisseur of working women. The book that you are about to read depends upon this eye, Munby's eye, the eye that observes. It is an eye which becomes ours as we resist or are drawn into complicity with its owner's voyeurism. But it is an absent eye, seen with but never seen itself – except for this brief verbal portrait of an eye, numbed with cocaine and cut by a surgeon's knife, when, at the age of nearly 70, Munby had a iridectomy to cure his glaucoma.

(The cocaine was poured into the eye to anaesthetize it before the iris was incised.) This was a pivotal moment: the voyeur faced with the possibility of sightlessness. Munby and his sight survived, however, and, true to character, he managed to persuade a housemaid at the clinic to confide 'her little story, and her views of service'.[2] Such little stories, and Munby's interventions in these lives, form the subject of my book.

Munby was a collector. His particular fascination was with the big-bodied working women whom he interviewed, befriended, sketched, photographed, catalogued and described in numerous diaries and journals. As has been relatively well known since the appearance of Derek Hudson's biography and Leonore Davidoff's path-breaking analysis, Munby's greatest experiment of all involved Hannah Cull-wick, a Shropshire domestic servant he met in London in 1854 (when they were both in their twenties) and married secretly after a clandes-tine relationship of two decades.[3] This cross-class marriage began with an attempt at living together as master and servant, husband and wife, but Cullwick soon left for Shropshire. They remained married, and in contact, but lived separately for most of the time. Munby's obsession with working women continued, but instead of contenting himself with interviews, he could now actually live the experience, first-hand, with his own 'rustic' wife. He dressed her like a 'peasant' in specially chosen, out-of-fashion clothing. He recorded his visits to this living museum, providing an ethnography of cottage life more intimate than that of any anthropologist. Intriguingly, it seems that Cullwick and Munby's relationship, though sexually charged, was celibate: they never had sexual intercourse.

Like the true fetishist, Munby accumulated items freighted with peculiar sexual meaning: the iron heel of a milkwoman's boot, a servant's discarded arm strap, parings from callused hands, even a satin cushion stuffed with his servant/wife's hair. The story that I will tell is one of strange possessions. But Munby went further than collecting things. He collected people, establishing relationships with disfigured women – never men – visiting them in their homes, presenting them with gifts of food, money and medical attention, and providing (as we shall see) rather sadistic human contact. The Bermondsey sack-girls who objected to having their photographs taken – 'they thinks it's witchcraft, or somethink' – were wiser than Munby thought.[4]

As a number of talented critics have shown, Munby was particu-larly alert to the complex interactions of gender, race and class in nineteenth-century Britain.[5] The whole of his oeuvre – a vast archive of diaries, letters, photographs, poems and sketches – is concerned with infraction and contrast: the daily marring of feminine ideals through bodily exertion, dirt and deformity. This book is a study of Munby's women (the objectification is deliberate), teasing out the implications of his fascination with transgression. My focus is on both the disruption and the construction of Victorian ideologies; it is an attempt to write in ambiguities, slippages and subversions. But my argument will be that although Munby was constantly disrupting the feminine ideal (small, fair, weak, smooth, well-formed) with notions of largeness, blackness, strength, coarseness and deformity, the psychological effect was actually to increase the power of the absent image.

As you turn the pages of *Watching Hannah*, you will encounter elements of classic horror. Barbara Creed has explained the viewing strategies available to audiences of horror films: 'By not-looking, the spectator is able momentarily to withdraw identification from the image on the screen in order to reconstruct the boundary between self and screen and reconstitute the "self" which is threatened with disintegration.'[6] As the reader/viewer (for there are visual as well as written images), you can distance yourself through the knowledge of fictive historical representation and perhaps look away or skip the page – though you will be ambushed from time to time. Through the very (fictive) power of historical representation, you will continually be in danger of becoming enmeshed in this story of voyeurism and fetishism.

At first glance, this book may seem a graphic instance of the reconfirmation that the gaze is male, with woman as the object and man as the bearer of the look. It may well be read in terms of a risky potential triple scopophilia – the power and pleasure of looking for three subjects: Munby, this male writer and the male reader/viewer. The object is woman, and the objective is the exploration of Munby's strategies of staging woman's 'to-be-looked-at-ness'.[7] Indeed, the reader, like this writer, may be both seduced and repelled by the sheer horror and skill of the voyeur's craft. As several critics have pointed out, the great danger in the replication of powerful racial and sexual images and stereotypes is that the mere act of reproduction will reinforce the very attitudes and power relations that it is the intention to critique.[8] And when – as in *Watching Hannah* – the textual and the visual combine, the impact can be exponential. Gentle irony is not always the most effective destabilizer.

But it is a risk that I am prepared to take, believing that, as with theories of film spectatorship, readings will be heterogeneous rather than unitary. We are passing through a *fin de siècle*, but it is a different one to the long historical moment described in this text – and temporal difference is a great distancer. Given the varied readings of gender, class, sexuality, academic discipline, race, age and the variously inscribed identities of those who might pick up this book, I would anticipate a multiplicity of reactions – what Christine Gledhill has termed 'pleasurable negotiations' – rather than simple closure.[9]

Indeed, those worried about closure or suspicious of authorial intent should take heart from the multiple readings of the historians, literary critics, art historians and sociologists who have negotiated the same archival material that I have employed in my staging. For Munby's archive has been mined for the story of the double life of a friend of the Victorian 'literary and artistic greats' (Hudson), for 'realistic' representations of working women (Hiley and John), as an account of the interactions between sex and gender in Victorian England (Davidoff), as a documentary source for the life and attitudes of a domestic servant (Stanley), as a telling instance of the imbrication of race and empire in private desires and domestic interactions (Pollock and McClintock), as a site for a feminist re-reading of the Victorian bourgeois white male (Pollock again), and – as I write this preface – for the rehabilitation of Munby as an English *flâneur* (Allen).[10] As Carol Mavor has observed, Hannah Cullwick has either remained invisible or has variously been presented as victim, heroine, invention and textual construct. Hannah has been both 'ordinary' (Stanley) and 'extraordinary' (Mavor). Heather Dawkins and Anne McClintock were interested in Cullwick's power of agency in a relationship based on extreme male control. Carol Mavor engaged in a sexual relationship with the represented Hannah; archival research was an erotic encounter: '... the photographs (and the diaries), for me, are overflowing with sexuality, flesh, desire'; 'I am drawn to this missing picture: it represents Hannah's invisible flesh. I want to touch it. I caress the place of her absence with gloved fingers.'[11] In short, a range of academic practitioners have written the intellectual history of the last twenty years on the bodies of Hannah Cullwick and Munby's working women.

Although Munby was a master of early fetishism, sadomasochism and voyeurism, we will discover that it is very difficult to categorize him – to classify him as an early sexologist might. Was he a masochist before masochism? A sadist before sadism? A fetishist before fetishism? A master of voyeurism? A *flâneur* who was more than a *flâneur*? When Hudson wrote his biography, situating Munby's sexuality was a relatively simple exercise (although sex is hardly one of that book's preoccupations). The historiography of the 1960s and early 1970s presented what is now termed the repressive hypothesis: a bipolar interpretation of Victorian sexuality, drawing a rigid dichotomy between the respectable public face of prudery and silence and a dark underside of pornography and prostitution – captured perfectly in the title of another product of the period, Steven Marcus's remarkable book *The Other Victorians*.[12] Sex featured in this view, but as absent or hidden.[13] Hudson's *Munby, Man of Two Worlds* refers to its subject's 'strange double life', his 'hidden life'.[14] Munby, according to this rendering, moved uncomfortably between two separate spheres (a discomfort clearly shared by the biographer).

But this simple duality sits uneasily with a newer historiography which posits the multiplicities of Victorian sex, a quantum shift in interpretation inspired by the appearance of the controversial first volume of Michel Foucault's history of sexuality.[15] Foucault's argument was not for a silence about sex in the Victorian period, but for its opposite: 'a veritable discursive explosion'.[16] Even – especially – when sex was being repressed, it was being talked about. For Foucault, and for those who have been influenced by him, the Victorian period saw an outpouring of discussion and classification of sex – in the debates, surveys and legislation dealing with population, public health, women's and children's work, prostitution and venereal disease; in the copious medical-advice literature and advertisements concerning sexual matters. The Victorian period also saw the emergence of recognizably modern attitudes and definitions: the fashioning and self-fashioning of homosexuality and heterosexuality, its 'other'; the emergence of sexologists, who began to focus on sex as the centre of a person's identity and a means of classification; the increase in practice of birth control and reduction of family sizes; the rise of pornography. Foucault was not arguing for freedom of sexuality in the Victorian period – indeed, all sorts of controls and categorizations were being made – but there was certainly no silence about sex.[17]

In a recent piece on Victorian sexuality, Noel Annan referred to Munby as a Victorian without sexual regard for women: 'His interest was not sexual, not even sociological: it was compassionate.'[18] Munby's biographer claimed much the same. Munby's obsession with working women was 'compassionate'; 'his masculine urges were less powerful than the average.'[19] But it would be a mistake to equate lack of sexual intercourse with lack of interest in sex. We will see that most of Munby's interactions with working women, including his wife, were highly sexualized. The permeating sexuality that characterized Munby's communications demonstrates the usefulness of a

Foucaultian interpretation. Although he is scarcely mentioned in Peter Gay's history of bourgeois culture or Michael Mason's two-volume work on Victorian sexuality, I will suggest that Arthur Munby provides an important insight into Victorian male desires.[20]

Although some of the images in this book may be familiar to a few readers, my approach is different to other studies, and I have new stories to tell.[21] This is not simply the account of a compulsive observer and collector of working women and fetishist of hard-working female hands, of an associate of John Ruskin who secretly married a servant and who formed rather chilling relationships with noseless women – though this narrative is interesting enough in itself. Rather, it is something of an experiment in trafficking in history, art history and literary studies, a conscious effort to make use of visual imagery as well as words. It uses one man's fantasies as a way of exploring Victorian male culture, but has implications for several cultural histories. Chapter 1, 'Watching Hannah', sets the context, telling the intriguing story of Munby's relationships and obsessions. Chapter 2, 'Harriet's Nose', uses the absent nose (the noseless women) to detect cultural apprehensions in *fin-de-siècle* Europe. Chapter 3, 'Venus in Dirt', explores Cullwick and Munby's sadomasochistic relationship, his attempt to create the woman of his fantasies, fashioning her through the pen, the photograph, elaborate stagings and his own imagination. Chapter 4, 'Disordering Bodies', shows that it is possible to turn to Munby's representations of working women, the arresting images of female masculinity, to demonstrate the non-fixity of gender. Chapter 5, 'Dorothy's Hands', uses Munby's hand fetish to discuss male femininity. Chapter 6, 'Sexuating Arthur' (the word *sexuating* is borrowed from Carol Mavor), discusses the implications of our case study for notions of Victorian sexuality, exploring the strange blend of control and desire – the dispersed sexuality – that characterizes Munby's encounters. The Postscript argues that this working example of one man's way of seeing reveals wider male preoccupations with femininity, the body, deformity, masculinity and sexuality during a fascinating period of European history. After reading and viewing with Munby's eyes, it is difficult to see things quite the same way again.

1 Watching Hannah

I

The point of departure in this book is not exactly unfamiliar: the complex of attitudes associated with rather refined notions of Victorian femininity.[1] John Ruskin captured the essential elements perfectly in the bi-polarities of description in two oft-quoted lectures. Man was active: 'He is eminently the doer, the creator, the discoverer, the defender.' His sphere of activity, 'his rough work in the open world', was hardening (he is '*always* hardened'). The woman's realm, however, was the home, 'the place of Peace'. 'By her office, and place, she is protected from all danger and temptation.' Her 'power is for rule, not for battle'; 'her intellect is not for invention or creation, but for sweet ordering.' Woman's 'great function', in Ruskin's words, was 'Praise'.[2] He wrote of the complementarity of the sexes – 'each completes the other' – but this was a highly gendered correspondence. Man and woman were 'in nothing alike'.[3] Ruskin waxed poetically on chiselling or hammering boys into shape, as with a rock or a piece of bronze. 'But you cannot hammer a girl into anything. She grows as a flower does, – she will wither without sun.' 'Let her loose in the library, I say, as you do a fawn in a field.'[4] His languages of womanhood refer to perfection and 'highest refinement' of beauty, 'delicate strength', 'exquisite *right*ness', 'delight', 'perfect loveliness', 'innocence', 'majestic peace', 'majestic childishness', modesty, patience and purity.[5] 'She must be enduringly, incorruptibly good; instinctively, infallibly wise – wise, not for self-development, but for self-renunciation: wise, not that she may set herself above her husband, but that she may never fail from his side.'[6]

Lynda Nead has analyzed what she calls the norm of respectable femininity represented in George Elgar Hicks's triptych *Woman's Mission* (exhibited in 1863, a year before Ruskin's lecture), with woman guiding, comforting and supporting during the various stages of life (illus. 1–3). As Nead has pointed out, the female subjects of

1–3 The feminine ideal: guide, companion, comfort (G. E. Hicks, *Woman's Mission*, 1863).

4 'A modern goddess': illustration from *London Society* (1873) to the poem 'At a Modern Shrine':

'But I swear, my darling, that you
Are like poor Pygmalion's statue,
When just flushing with life's roseate suffusion …
I believe that, could I see a Grecian goddess
In a bodice
Poppy-hued, and skirts the colour of the wheat;
With a spray of lilac blossom
In her chastely-covered bosom,
I should find my British darling just as sweet.'

these three paintings portray woman as 'a unified and coherent category'. She, 'woman', is defined purely in terms of her relationships to men: 'young mother, dutiful wife and caring daughter'. She is the nurturer of males. Moreover, this representative of femininity is young – a youthful ideal emphasized by the aging of the males in the triptych (son, husband, father). In short, this powerful discourse of femininity presented woman as living her life in subordinate refinement.[7] And there were obvious implications for ideals of feminine beauty.

A lesser-known associate of Ruskin recorded his ideals of feminine beauty, writing in the 1860s of the 'lithe airy shape, the transcendent purity expressed in faultless manners, of the true lady'.[8] He was particularly charmed by the writer Anne Thackeray, who looked 'infinitely bright & spirituelle … all lithe and tremulous … her face & limbs as it were gleaming and flashing perpetually with the impulse of thought and strong feeling'. 'Surely', our informant confided to his diary, 'there is not another girl in England, so artless & intense, with such a charm of love & of power!'[9] Then, in the 1890s, he was similarly taken with a 'beautiful girl' of 'twenty or so'. She had a slight figure, small wrists, delicate hands, a 'singularly sweet and girlish face, with an aureole of golden curly hair around it, and a very fair complexion', large clear blue eyes, beautiful teeth 'and mobile expressive lips'. She possessed, he wrote, the face and figure not of a lady, 'yet refined looking and loveable in a high degree'. She was dainty and delicate, small and slender, a 'rosebud of a girl', a 'beautiful toy', a 'charming pet'.[10] Indeed, she was remarkably like the illustrated feminine ideal depicted in the journal *London Society* (1873), pale when not blushing, delicate, 'a modern goddess' (illus. 4).

Our observer, the civil servant and poet Arthur Munby, is central to this book. As we shall see, Munby's world is inexplicable without the ideological framework of the culture of Victorian femininity, but his interest and importance lies in the multiple ways in which he mentally crossed the boundaries so carefully mapped by his friend Ruskin. Indeed, Munby's examples of femininity relayed above were counter-poised against their opposites, which he also admired: 'the brawny bulk, the bold artless freedom, of the peasant girl', 'the tall, robust, bronzed woman'.[11] As Munby once expressed it, he was aware of both the 'strong-minded' and the 'pseudo-angelic' theories of women, but wanted to get 'beyond' them. He was interested in a definition of femininity which allowed (certainly) for humility, gentleness and patience, but also for 'strength' rather than 'weakness'.[12]

II

As intimated, Munby is not exactly unknown to historians. Their main interest in him has related to what his biographer rather delicately termed his 'compassionate feeling for working women'.[13] Munby was a compulsive voyeur of working women. He had his particular haunts: 'London Bridge, more than any place I know here, seems to be the great thoroughfare for young working women and girls,' he wrote in 1861.[14] He was right; it was calculated in 1857 that 85,690 people crossed the bridge in a mere twelve hours (illus. 5).[15] In 1863, Munby went to Epsom, to the Derby – captured in W. P. Frith's famous painting *Derby Day* (illus. 6) and described by the *Saturday Review* as a site where 'the endless varieties of the human species assembled within the radius of a mile and a half'.[16] Like many other amateur anthropologists, Munby went to observe the crowd, not the races. He sought out those he knew would be there: the gipsy girls; female tramps, foraging for empty bottles and food; and the racing-card girls. He met a female black-face minstrel in a beer tent and persuaded her to go with him to a photographer's booth so that he could take her picture for a shilling (illus. 7).[17] He went to the Queen's Review of Troops in Windsor Park – not for the soldiers, but to 'see the spectators'.[18] He travelled along the Thames by steamer, reflecting

5 'The Living Stream at London Bridge', *London Society* (1863).

6 Detail from W. P. Frith's painting *Derby Day*, 1858.

7 'Female "Nigger" [street dancer] taken at Epsom Derby Day 1863. Aged 23: married.'

that 'these river steamers are the best place for seeing the various ugliness, the infinite and pathetic commonplace, the general good behaviour, of the lower classes of London.'[19] One of the attractions of London, 'the Modern Babylon', was the close juxtaposition of rich and poor.[20] One late afternoon in July, Munby counted over a hundred homeless women in St James's Park, dressed in 'filthy draggled muslins' (which had once been someone's finery). They were a silent 'prostrate crowd', women too 'low' to even get a living by prostitution. And this was with 'Carlton House Terrace and Westminster Abbey looking down at them, and infinite welldrest citizens passing by on the other side'.[21]

Munby also traversed what have been termed London's erotic neighbourhoods, the theatrical areas of the city, with their attendant zones of prostitution and trade in erotica.[22] In just one week of wandering the streets in 1862, he encountered an artist's model who thought nothing of posing naked, observed a milkwoman ('vacant as a cabhorse') and a dustwoman, and questioned some female black-face minstrels and two homeless women, once again too ragged and dirty to earn a living as prostitutes, whom he 'dismissed ... with some advice and a sixpence'.[23] He trailed a milkwoman on her round from Bond Street to Whitehall – watching and following her to Piccadilly: 'I studied her more or less all the way, chiefly from across the street.' He was fascinated by her invisibility to passers-by as she did her round; by the contrast between the 'statuesque features' of her face and her elephantine body; and by the manner in which she was ignored while all eyes turned to the ladies in their carriages and 'every peacock prostitute' she passed on her route. He contrasted her 'rustic unconscious purity' with the vice of Coventry Street, 'that Babel of gay men and tawdry evil women'. He observed her window-shopping after she had made her last delivery. And he followed her back to her master's, tracking her for almost an hour.[24]

Munby has been described as a *flâneur*, wandering the city and observing women as they went about their work: milkwomen, dust-women and domestic servants.[25] However, he did not confine his studies to the great conurbations; his archives document forays into most parts of rural England and the mining areas of the Black Country and the North. His quarry also included colliers, nailer-girls, fish-erwomen, field workers and even dye-house girls with their faces and arms stained indigo, sky-blue and violet.[26] In 1865, he visited the coal pits, coke ovens, blast furnaces and brickworks of the Blaenavon Valley. He described and sketched the dust-covered 'girls' of the brick kilns, who wore ragged smocks that reached 'just below the knee', revealing either cotton trousers or stocking-clad legs in large boots. These young workers wore leather pads to hold the bricks, and Munby noticed that one of the shovellers, who was not wearing pads, was picking at her hand. This provided him with the opportunity to offer to cut the calluses from her hand – which she accepted – and to write: '... the knife cut slowly through the thick horn of this girlish hand.' He then walked to the coke ovens, where a large number of young women were employed digging and sifting coke, and emptying ironstone out of railway trucks. Nearby were the blast furnaces, which also employed female labour to fill and wheel barrows, but mostly to break lumps of ironstone. These women, who worked thus twelve hours a day, wielding large hammers, were coloured by the stone they broke: yellow-grey with the ironstone, or red with Northumbrian ore.[27]

Nor was he a distanced viewer. Munby quizzed his subjects, often in dialect, seeking out their 'histories'.[28] Power was everything in his

8 Hannah Poynter, ballast digger.

encounters. As he explained, it was easy to get these women to talk:

… such girls always do: deep down in the shifting mass of the people, their own names and histories have for them nothing private or sacred; they are accustomed to be close questioned about themselves by mistresses, and to be called Ann or Mary by any one who chooses to address them. To be asked bluntly 'What is your name?' or 'How old are you?' by a stranger does not seem to them at all offensive or impertinent.[29]

He 'befriended' a Medway navvy, Hannah Poynter, a tanned and muscular woman who earned her living digging clay from a quarry for ships' ballast (illus. 8). In 1867, he sat in Poynter's two-roomed cottage while she breastfed her baby and washed in a basin on the dresser ('It was not the first or second time that I had seen fair Hannah at her toilette'). Munby was able to give free reign to his theories about the compatibility between femininity and hard labour. Here was a case in which a woman, 'sweet and motherly', could, at the same time, work with a pick 'like a navvy'. Hard physical labour was not

20

necessarily degrading. He wrote of the contrast between snowy breasts and sunburnt faces; brown fingers pressed against a 'full milky bosom'. Munby asked Poynter where her pick was: '"In the bedroom, Sir", said she, quietly ... and she opened the inner door.' He then saw the room – containing a bed, chair and clothes box – where her dead child had been laid out the last time he had visited. Munby's subjects did not merely talk to him; they let him into their cottages, their bedrooms ... and their pain. And all the time he was 'Sir'.[30]

Munby was alert to the possibility of deception, but was philosophical about the situation: 'On the whole, my view of such narratives is simply, that if they are true they are worth knowing; and if not, they have at least gratified the imagination with a momentary semblance of romance.'[31] There is no escaping the arrogance of class assumption. As Munby noted in the midst of his description of an encounter with a female telegraph clerk,

The real proof of a (conventional) inferiority – accepted generally with touching unconsciousness – is when a woman talks freely to you, and answers your questions (the delicacy of which is often quite superfluous) about herself and her belongings, and asks no questions of you in return.[32]

Nor can we ignore his cynicism and detachment; he treated his subjects as specimens for amusement. He reserved most disdain for shopgirls and milliners, conceiving them as a class of their own, between the reserve of a lady and the vulgarity of a servant. He was amused by one woman's grammatical mistakes and her 'perfect naiveté'. He found it refreshing that a 'girl' like that opened up the 'little history of her life' to a total stranger. She was honest and simple-minded. Women of his class would never have behaved in that way.[33]

Unlike the *flâneur*, Munby breached distance through physical contact. The handshake, and the visual assessment which accompanied it, determined the marital status and class of the owner of the hand. He went to the Foresters' Day at Crystal Palace in 1860 and, amidst tens of thousands of working people, located a servant – the reputedly downwardly mobile daughter of a vicar – with hands the size of a 'six foot bricklayer': '... oh, ye ballroom partners, what a breadth of massive flesh it was to grasp!' The young woman allowed her acquaintance to revel in their contrasts, traversing the boundaries of gender and class:

We read in novels, how the highborn hero receives in his broad palm the little white hand of his rustic love: well, here is the rustic maiden & here the big bearded hero – and lo, *his* is the 'small white' hand, and *hers* the big broad palm which his comparatively slender fingers span with difficulty.[34]

He visited the International Exhibition of 1862 and headed for the machinery annexe to examine the women at work on the cotton and muslin machines. His comments give a good idea of the initial direction of his glance: their hands (most were ringless: unmarried); their bodies (young and of average size and 'comeliness'). Munby's attention was on the operatives, not the machinery. One of the women gave the viewers a short lecture on machine work:

Here was an untaught young woman in a cotton frock and sacking apron, standing in the midst of a circle of well drest men, and talking to them about machinery; and with as much intelligence and self command & blunt straight forwardness & freedom of gesture (for she used her hands and bare arms as indexes of meaning) as if she had been a work*man*.

Munby was able to talk to this woman, establishing, as indeed he suspected, that the exhibition did not really reflect Lancashire cotton work. The women's boss had bought them new frocks for the show. Men were working the mules in the exhibition whereas in Manchester piecing was women's work. Munby's informant explained why: '... ye know t' lasses works barefoot and burlegged, and when they stoop ovver t' mule ye can see ever sae far up t' calf a't leg; and wer used te that i't mill, but masters thought it wouldn't do here.'[35] Munby returned to the exhibition at a later date and resumed his conversation, steering it, in his practiced manner, to more intimate matters. It transpired that the woman's husband had been in America for several years; 'she didn't like her anomalous position – neither wife nor maid.' She also told him that she, and most of the women operatives in the machinery exhibit, had been propositioned by male spectators; 'Be off, or Ah'll kick your arse,' one woman had responded.[36] Munby constructed his own exhibits at the Exhibition. He watched the elegant gentlefolk who thought that they were viewers rather than viewed, enjoying the contrast between them and the operatives. He even lingered at the end of the day to watch the employees lining up to be paid – another unauthorized exhibit.[37]

Such activity was by no means unusual in the nineteenth century. 'We have no need to go abroad to study ethnology', a contributor to Charles Dickens's *Household Words* wrote in 1855; 'A walk through the streets of London will show us specimens of every human variety known.' 'Life, in all its boundless power of joy and suffering – this is the great picture-book to be read in London streets.'[38] A contributor to *London Society* wrote similarly of the 'ever-shifting diorama' of the streets, a 'moving picture gallery'.[39] It is instructive to compare Munby to another chronicler of labouring life, Henry Mayhew. Like

Munby, Mayhew 'relayed' the life stories of the people as seamless histories, when they were in fact narratives crafted from a series of questions and responses. Like Munby, he tapped into narratives that his informants had already constructed from tropes of popular literature: for Munby, the upper- or middle-class woman fallen into a life of degradation; for Mayhew, the picaresque hero. As with Munby, there was exchange of money: experience purchased or told in the hope of recompense. There were similar sexual subtexts to both men's wanderings. When they talked to women, they bought their stories rather than their bodies, but these women were used to being approached by social superiors for sex. Sex lurked as an unspoken possibility. For both men, their quarry was an 'other'.[40]

As we shall see, photography was central to Munby's interaction with his working-class subjects. They were interesting exhibits, to be posed, discussed and captured in image (illus. 9–13). Munby's attitude is reflected in his musings in 1860 over the photographing of the pitwoman Margaret Hunter (illus. 14). Hunter remained impassive through the entire process, even when she was handed the obligatory

9 Maid of all work, Westminster Bridge Road, 1861.

10 Bermondsey sackmaker.

11, 12 Fishing women: These women worked in the fishing industry in Filey and Flamborough (North Yorkshire/Humberside); they also climbed up and down high cliffs to collect bait and driftwood (see Chapter 4). The woman with the bundle on her head, and seated in the second photograph, is Annie Barn; the other woman is her sister-in-law: 'Taken one day at noon, as they came home alone, to dinner, from their work at the herring house. It was hung up over the fireplace in the cottage till Annie's mother gave it to me. Filey 1867'.

13 Kent farm servant, 1863.

14 Margaret Hunter,
pitwoman, 1862.

shilling, two-thirds of a day's wage: 'You might have gone up to her, examined her with hand and eye, & talked over her various "points", and she would have shown no more emotion than a horse or a dog.'[41] Such little theatres of cold exhibiting lurked behind the black-and-white image of the *carte*.

III

The long relationship between Arthur Munby and the servant Hannah Cullwick (illus. 15) went through different phases. First, there was the secret courtship. He would arrange to walk past her place of work on a day when she would be particularly dirty so that he could 'see her in her dirt'. They might meet in the street at dusk.[42] She would visit him in his rooms; '… the maiden comes to the man', as Munby put it, 'and not the man to the maiden.' If he had visited her openly at her place of service, it would have caused scandal because of the gap in their social standing, whereas her same lowliness permitted her to visit him as a servant, without comment.[43]

15 Hannah Cullwick as general servant to a tradesman in Kilburn in 1860. Note the exposure of the arms and hands.

Usually, she would visit on Sundays, cooking for him and then cleaning up afterwards, sitting him on her lap, washing his feet, making cigarettes while he read to her.[44] Sometimes, she demonstrated her strength by lifting either her lover or the coal box. Sometimes, she licked his boots.[45] On at least one occasion in 1862, she used her face as a duster, rubbing her cheeks on some dirty boxes of Munby's until her face was black.[46] At times, she was so tired from her labours that she fell asleep as soon as she arrived at his house; Munby once recorded Cullwick crying in her sleep from sheer exhaustion.[47]

During this period, it was always possible that Munby would marry someone of his own class. Cullwick wrote that the prospect 'seem'd to choke me, & as if it'd kill me to see it come off'. She contemplated continuing the relationship as a servant in his married household, showing her devotion through work: '... we should show our love silently.' But she thought that this would be unfair to his wife.[48]

Then there was the secret marriage when Cullwick moved in with Munby and lived with him as both wife and servant; all but his closest friends thought that she was his servant rather than his wife. Indeed, she acted as a charwoman for other tenants in the building. During this phase, Munby and Cullwick lived daily with the juxtaposition of their respective worlds: 'Everyday, I see my darling in her housemaid's dress at breakfast.'[49] There was no respite – the pressure for Cullwick must have been unbearable. As Munby wrote, '... it was part of the programme, that she should scour the stairs "in her dirt", so as to look as unattractive as might be, in that public employment.'[50] It is difficult to know how Cullwick felt about this phase of their relationship. Because she lived with Munby, she no longer wrote him letters or kept her diary.

Munby's diaries in London during the early years of their marriage consist of a series of observations about Cullwick's dirty work, and references to his own social rounds: 'Home at 6 to dress: to Queen Anne Street by 7.30, and dined with the Hensleigh Wedgwoods. Miss W., Edmund Maurice & wife, the Litchfields, a Mr. Scott. Pleasant and clever talk. Home on foot by 11.45.'[51] When he socialized with his cultured acquaintances, he took secret satisfaction in the shock they would experience if they knew his true situation: '... my dear people, what will you do to me when you come to know that I am the husband of a common servant' (note the shift in possession: he is a servant's husband).[52] He could stage meetings (though *meeting* is scarcely the right word if any interaction is implied) between friend and dirty servant. There is a memorable description of light streaming through the parlour window, illuminating all the dust and confusion in front of the hearth (the centre of the Victorian home) and revealing, amidst this disorder, 'the dirtiest object of all – a woman', a blackened Cullwick on her hands and knees among doormats and dustpans, and crawling out of the room to avoid disturbing her master's visitor. And there is Munby's recorded delight that the visitor 'never once deigned to notice that humble creature on the floor'.[53]

On another occasion, Munby and the antiquarian Edward Peacock talked archaeology, philosophy and the latter's novel, and recited poetry and ballads, while the servant cleared away, and left the room backwards ('for she always backs out of a room before gentlefolks'). Peacock held forth about the scene in his novel involving a servant and her master, noting how, 'unhappily', servants had 'not culture' to describe their lives. Munby noted his visitor's obliviousness to the real servant's presence. He took 'no more notice of her ... than if she had been a dog'; 'he noted not her countenance nor her movements: nor knew that she, without any culture at all, has described her own life effectively for nearly thirty years.' The delicious irony of the situation was not lost on Munby. Here was a novelist, an expert on manorial rights and local history, discussing rustic scenes and the lives of servants, yet unconscious of the servant in front of him.[54]

Then there was the longest and final phase in Munby and Cullwick's relationship: the commuting marriage. It is difficult to know what provoked the separation. One of Cullwick's letters implies that the initiative was his: 'I see that you love me as much as ever your nature will let you, & I also see that you enjoy being alone as a bachelor & having no inclination like other men for a wife its decidedly better that you shouldn't be bothered with one about you.'[55] She also suggested that she had not envisaged their relationship ending up in that way, and chided herself for her innocence. She should have been more alert to the implications of their 'long engagement': '... tho I didn't expect this sort of suffering – to be alone in the world – that is of all things the worst thing that a woman can have to endure'.[56]

During this stage, the marriage was only partially secret. They did not conceal it from the rural community in which Cullwick lived; her friends, neighbours and family knew about it. Shame was class-based; there was no need for secrecy in the Shropshire village, for there was no-one there who counted: 'This social anomaly, indeed, could not exist in an ordinary rural village. But at Hadley, there are no gentry, to peer and gossip and give a cue to the tradesfolk; and the labourers are mostly forgemen and colliers, who care nothing for social anomalies.'[57] But the marriage was a secret in Munby's sphere of operation.

Munby's experiment is inexplicable without realizing the context:

the place of the rural in English ideology. For Munby, as for so many of his contemporaries, the rural signified the tranquillity of a lost age in the face of change. It was represented by the picturesque village with labourers at the inn door, women at the parish pump and children playing in the street. It was gables, shady trees, water butts, brooms, geranium pots and wicker cages.[58] Part of Cullwick's appeal for Munby was her rural background. Indeed, in 1873, when he told a friend of his predicament, he omitted the detail of Cullwick's humiliating charring 'which to him might have seemed to mar the pure ideal of a rustic sweetheart'.[59] Significantly, Cullwick was a gleaner in her later cottage phase. Gleaners were central to the iconography of rural romanticism and nostalgia (illus. 16). For Munby, gleaning permitted yet another opportunity to combine rural idealization with the fetishism of the marks of rugged labour on the female body. In one memorable description, Cullwick is out in the fields with two of her neighbour's children, 'good little girls, but ragged and dirty':

16 Hannah Cullwick, peasant: photograph taken in Newport, Shropshire (Salop), 1872. Note the pastoral backdrop, rolled-up sleeves, exposed legs and boots.

29

'Hannah, in her old hood bonnet, and short cotton frock, and sack apron and leasing bag, and my strong boots, with her bronzed rustic face, and her bare arms and hands all soiled with earth and scratched with briars'. This description provided an opportunity for Munby's voyeuristic imagery of the double interactions of power: the male class superior versus the female social inferior. A farmer confronted Cullwick. She expected to be reprimanded, and stood deferentially before him 'as Ruth stood before Boaz'. But the man was kind; he saw 'her humble dress and her hardworking hands'. Cullwick called him 'Sir' and curtsied, and (the authorial fiction of presence) blushed 'with pleasure'. The supra-text was of course that, unknown to the farmer, this poor woman was married to a gentleman, and that Munby, the author of the note describing this act of obeisance and kindly exercise of authority, was the farmer's social superior.[60]

Cullwick and Munby went through such repetitive rituals year after year – even when they were in their 60s and 70s. Munby's journals contain the same descriptions of clothing, toilette and daily rituals, delight in contrasts, reports of cross-class interaction, portraits of dirt and cleaning, stories from the past, justifications of their relationship:

'... as I said to you when you first know'd me, an' I was scullion at Woodcote ... I was scouring the kitchen floor on my hands an' knees, when them thoughts come in my head, as I should be prouder at been your *slave*, nor to be raised so as to be thought a equal – And I've always stuck to that', she added. Yes, she has always stuck to that; and by that very humility and serviceableness, has increased a thousand fold the reverence and honour which her husband has always felt for her lowly condition, contrasted as it is so strongly with her personal beauty and with the purity and unchanging faithfulness of her love.[61]

It was a game that Cullwick willingly played. She knew instinctively what Munby wanted to hear. During one of his visits in 1891, she told her husband of the visit of the new curate: '"...an' he *would* shake hands wi' me. Eh, his hand is small and thin!" she added, looking down at her own large rugged hand and mutilated thumb.'[62] Through Cullwick's descriptions and his own physical presence at the site of the encounter between his wife and the curate – 'Her kitchen ... looked just as it was when the Curate saw it'[63] – Munby was able to recreate the experience as a voyeur, doubtless drawing on a myriad of similar interactions. Thus recorded in his journal, he was able, by reading, to conjure up such episodes at whim.

In another journal entry, Munby recalled the visit of Miss Half-penny, the curate's landlady. Cullwick left the door ajar so that Munby could witness the interaction between the socially aspiring tradesman's daughter (said to have designs on the curate) and Hannah, a servant, married to Halfpenny's social superior. The hapless woman, not aware that she had walked onto a private stage, was the perfect foil to the servant/wife's performance. Cullwick delighted in shocking the rather prim young woman with her detailed descriptions of the couple's relationship and their daily routines – including the information that she washed herself all over once a week, 'an he helps me to it, so he knows as I *are* clean all over'.[64] As Munby observed,

… when brought face to face with women who are her superiors but are not ladies, she takes a malicious pleasure in appearing vulgar and ignorant, and in telling out the details of her hard work and her humble experience with a frankness that is meant to disgust and repel these worthies.[65]

Of course, Cullwick was performing for Munby as well as for her unsuspecting visitor. Although it has the appearance of a verbatim report, the final script that we have – some 35 pages of prose – would have been crafted later, based on what Munby heard (he could not actually see the meeting) and Cullwick's own descriptions. It is a carefully constructed rehearsal of the usual themes of their relationship.[66]

Sometimes, Munby used sketches to add to the voyeurism. In 1901, when in his 70s, he watched, sketched and described Cullwick talking to a well-dressed man outside her cottage. The sketch (illus. 17) exaggerates the burly, blackened working woman (the gentler sex) alongside the slender man. Her hands are monstrously overstated, while the man's are hidden in his pockets. This episode is drawn and described in Munby's journal as an encounter between superior and inferior. If we had only the sketch to go on, we might well think that the man was a gentleman, perhaps Munby himself. In fact, the journal explains with savoured irony, the man was merely the village grocer, a social subordinate to the husband of the woman he had treated as his inferior. Munby relished such twists.[67]

The layers of voyeurism are unrelenting, heightened by Munby's use of the third person. We have Cullwick's accounts of her daily degradation, sent to her husband in letters and summarized in his journal entries: 'She has just got in 28 cwt. (nearly 1½ ton) of coals, with her own hands ... the sweat running down her black face.'[68] We watch Munby watching himself watching Hannah undressing and dressing, cleaning the steps, getting in coal for the fire, collecting dung off the roads (note the signifiers of degradation), foraging for wood, selling fish at market. We watch Munby watching others watching Cullwick. Better still, Munby watches others ignoring, *not watching*, disdaining his working wife.

17 Hannah Cullwick and the village grocer, 1901: 'Such a woman, so clad, was a piquant contrast to the man.'

'I'm goin to clean my doorsteps, Massa, if you'd like to see me.' 'Certainly, my dear', says he; and stands in his lofty manner at the cottage door, while his buxom wife, kneeling at his feet, scours her doorsteps with vigorous arms, and with a skill that shows she is no novice in that art. First she washes the mud off with a wet cloth, rinsing it and wringing it tight in the dirty water of her pail; then she rubs the yellow hearth stone all over each step; then, with a cleaner wet cloth, she leads the tone of yellow over the step, until it is smooth and uniform in colour. Finally, she kneels in the road, and washes the bricks below the lowest step. 'Don't they look nice?' she says proudly, lifting her head and looking up at him, with cheeks reddened by the air and exercise. But he is thinking of her, how well she looks at that lowly and useful labour: wearing her blue cotton frock, her coarse harden apron, her large white servant's cap, her husband's strong laced boots; her bare arms ruddy, her whole frame robust and serviceable and healthful and rustic. But two 'swells' in a smart yellow gig, who stop close by ... have no such thoughts: they disdain to look down at that humble woman who is all the world to the man in the doorway.[69]

Or Munby mentally distances himself, seeing himself and Cullwick as others might see them – walking down the street, standing together at the station or with her sitting between his knees and telling him about the vicar's visit: '… you see, I was upstairs doin the bedroom, an' I had on my blue cotton frock and coarse apron, an' nothink on my head.'[70] The multiple layers of possibility are evident in an entry in Munby's journal where he describes a photograph of his wife – bare-armed apart from the trade-mark wrist-strap – sitting on a wall like 'a peasant woman waiting for a job' (illus. 18). As he explained, the photograph, which, because of its subject matter, could not be shown publicly, was displayed next to the living item. The third layer of voyeurism was provided by Munby's description of the bizarre double image.[71]

Such narrations provided occasion after occasion for Munby's favoured themes of dominance and submission, attainment of nobility through servitude, and what he saw as the kaleidoscope of class difference refracted around the figure of his servant wife (compare illus. 19 and 20): 'And again, half undrest, she looked as tender and sweet as a maiden. So kaleidoscopic is her life. But she said "Massa, feel how rough my hands are!"'[72] Although he held the power, he indulged in a fantasy of powerlessness in the face of womanly might:

18 Hannah Cullwick aged 62: 'The latest and best photograph of his wife as she now is: wearing her old hood bonnet, her short cotton frock, her coarse apron and strong boots; her fine muscular arms bare, and the strap on her wrist. On a low wall she sits, a peasant woman waiting for a job.' Obviously, the picture was taken in a studio.

19 Hannah Cullwick as a lady: 'This is a portrait of Her which my friend D. G. Rossetti admired so warmly, and wished for a copy of it, when he saw it in 1862 at my chambers in the Temple. "It is a beautiful face", he said, "a remarkable face indeed; I should like to know that lady."'

20 Hannah Cullwick as a servant: a working woman's hands. Munby carried this image around with him in a travelling case.

'As for her idle and useless husband, he looked on, powerless and admiring, at the public display of his black wife's strength and skill ... "Is my face *terribly* black?" she asked, standing at the door, in full view of every one.'[73]

Sometimes, they went away together as man and wife, with Cullwick as a lady: 'The gleaner, the fishwoman, the servant of all work, had to be turned into a lady, or at least into the semblance of a lady, for twenty four hours.'[74] The role-playing, the masquerade, was always Cullwick's: 'I'm Cinderella again now, and only yesterday I was at the ball!'[75] Munby did not cross-dress, pass or disguise. It was Cullwick who had to traverse class in a superficially simple but in fact very complex round of acting which involved not only public display but also private interaction within the household. As Cullwick once put it, 'How nice it is to be your wife and servant too! It's like a *play*, only better nor all the plays that ever was wrote.'[76] Sometimes, the transformation would be a more private masquerade. One evening in 1887, Cullwick retired upstairs and returned dressed as a lady in muslin and lace, with silver and gold jewellery: 'I thought you should see me as a lady again, for once!'[77] Later, when she resisted playing the role of a lady, Munby took solace in the fantasy that she could 'assume the part without an effort' if her 'husband insisted'.[78]

One of Munby's unpublished poems promised an end to the masquerade. A time would come when the gentleman would take his humble wife by her rough hands and declare their secret to his proud friends.[79] But it never happened. The masquerade only ended with Cullwick's death in 1909.

IV

In 1859 Arthur Munby came across two human skins exhibited at an 'Institute of Anatomy'. He passed quickly over the description of the male hide, but lingered over the female exhibit:

The woman's skin was quite perfect from head to foot: it was slit down the back, and hung loosely on a wooden cross, in hideous mockery of the living figure. It was much thinner than the man's, but as thick as a stout glove. It was horrible to look at the face – it was like a leather mask, every feature perfect, yet hanging helpless & collapsed – the nose awry, the lips drooping, the eyes wide and empty. The head too was covered with brown hair, parted in the middle, and even plaited down the cheeks as in life: and under it were two little round parchment ears. The flesh & bones had been withdrawn from the hands apparently without cutting: they were like two gloves, dry &

wrinkled, & with the nail at the end of each finger. I lifted the stiff hand, & touched the dusty hair: to think what she had been, & what she was! One's thoughts might well play Hamlet, with such a theme. Only, *who* she was, no one knew: a *young* woman evidently – she died, perhaps, in some hospital; and after death her corpse was flayed, and her skin was sold and passed from hand to hand – for years, till she was bought and hung up to be looked at.

There are sentimental horrors, religious horrors, in such a sight: but it is enough to have seen, tanned like oxhide and stretched on two poles for all to handle and gaze at from year to year, *a woman's skin*.[80]

This was the ultimate objectification: surfaces paraded; a woman's skin in the control of strangers, able to be handled and gazed upon, 'sold and passed from hand to hand – for years'. And the imagination could construct its former occupant at will. Fantasy could reign. Munby's fascination with women's bodies, his fetishism and objectification, reached its logical conclusion in that moment he handled an anonymous woman's flayed skin: the awry nose, plaited hair, glove-like hands (mummified traces of an absent femininity), the imagery of corpses and masks, the repeated references to hands and to looking and touching, the theme of subverted perfection. It is only a short description, but it contains many of the horrors in the pages that follow.

2 Harriet's Nose: Horror, Bodily De-formation and Femininity

I

This story has many possible beginnings. I would have liked to have started with a photograph, a shocking image. But the appropriate photographs have vanished from what is otherwise an extensive collection. So perhaps I should have begun with a blank, a simple rectangle where the photograph should have been, an absent image all the more powerful for its non-appearance. Roland Barthes has written eloquently of the 'punctum', an incongruous part of a photograph, a minor detail at which the viewer can pick away, destabilizing the power of the image. The punctum disturbs, wounds, pricks, stings, shocks.[1] But the punctum in my image would have been its very absence.

Since the subject of this chapter is an absent nose, we could also begin with a literary reference.[2] With Hugo's nose, for example. Hugo, the fictional male narrator in Emily de Laszowska's *The Tragedy of a Nose* (1898), owes his awe-inspiring beauty to his nose, the 'central gem' in a 'lovely' profile. Hugo's beauty is established in the opening lines of the novella, and his nose determines his destiny: 'I felt it incumbent on me to live up to my nose.' In particular, it held great attraction for the opposite sex: 'Of course my beauty met with all the usual favour of recognition from poets, painters, sculptors and women – women especially.' Predictably, Hugo's tragedy hinges on the fate of his proboscis. He loses his nose in a duel – 'my nose, my beautiful nose, the pride of my face, and the hitherto idol of my existence, had been taken from me by a ruthless butcher hand.' Miraculously, however, the missing nose is recovered and restored by a celebrated Viennese surgeon. Even more astonishingly, Hugo had also severed his opponent's nose, and – unbeknown to anyone – the retrievers had confused the respective body parts, so that when the restorative surgery had healed, and Hugo's bandages were removed, he was wearing the nose of his enemy:

I cast an agonised glance upon my reflection; and, as I gazed, I felt and saw my blood all receding from my face, leaving it blanched and livid as the face of a corpse. The eyes that were looking out at me with that expression of frozen horror, were indeed my own, and the lips, though drawn and distorted by mental anguish, had the old familiar graceful curve; the ears as of yore sat close to my head like twin shells moulded there by a sculptor's hand; but my chief feature, the nose – oh, how shall I say it? – was not my own. It was a stranger, a parasite, an alien intruder, which wise and harmonious Nature could never have placed there in conjunction with those other features; and yet, not a stranger either, worse than that, a thousand times worse, for it was the nose of my deadliest enemy – of Wenzel Wondraczek!

Thereafter, Hugo suffers the indignity of facial incongruity. Consistent ugliness was preferable, he argued, to the caricature of his face: his handsome classical profile subverted by its 'outrageously turned-up snub nose'. His fortune follows the fate of his nose: '... to be a ridiculous man is necessarily to be an unfortunate and unsuccessful one.' His enemy, on the other hand, who had undergone identical surgery, had been transformed by the acquisition of Hugo's faultlessly elegant nose:

A feature like that alone was sufficient to confer beauty and distinction upon all the rest, as a single diamond of pure water ennobles the most sordid surroundings. Yes, there could be no doubt that Wenzel Wondraczek might now without exaggeration be called a fine-looking man, and it was I who, against my will, had made him so.

Wenzel stole Hugo's nose, his sweetheart and his happiness.[3]

Nikolai Gogol has written a much-cited story about another missing nose. The self-styled 'Major' Kovalyov awakes one morning to discover that his nose has disappeared: '... instead of a fairly presentable and reasonably sized nose, all he saw was an absolutely preposterous smooth flat space.' Kovalyov is acutely aware of the loss of his nose. His disfigurement destroys his confidence in pursuing pretty women. He wanders the streets, hiding his face behind a handkerchief. The loss of a nose is the greatest disfigurement, he argues, for it erases a man's character: 'If I'd lost an arm or leg it wouldn't be so bad. Even without any *ears* things wouldn't be very pleasant, but it wouldn't be the end of the world. A man without a nose, though, is God knows what, neither fish nor fowl.'[4]

The story I will eventually tell is that of a woman's nose, so let us begin again with a cross-class encounter between a cultured civil servant (and poet) and a poor working woman, a crossing of lives in nineteenth-century London, recorded by the man, Arthur Munby:

'Well Mary, your face looks quite nice now' – 'Yes Sir it's a deal better, if only I get a nose put on' – 'And when you've got a nose, what will you do?' 'Well Sir, when I've got my nose, I think I shall go into service'. 'How? But won't they find out that you've got a false nose?' 'No Sir, I expect not – they won't see the joining. My nose will be fastened on with a hook, and I can take it off when I like!' 'And how long have you been without a nose?' 'Four years Sir: it'll seem quite strange to have one again.'[5]

The woman was eighteen-year-old Mary Anne Bell. She had cancer which had eaten away her nose, leaving a gap into the mouth and throat. When the hole healed, it shrank to the size of a sixpence (the observation is Munby's): 'The absence of a nose makes her face look very much like an ape's, and shows how essentially human such a feature is.' Not only had the absence of a nose erased femininity; it had also removed this living body's visible humanity. It was a reminder of evolutionary origins. There is little compassion in Munby's description. His response was more one of amused curiosity. The nature of the relationship is clear from the languages of their interaction: she is 'Mary', and he is 'Sir'. She was motivated by the hope that this man with money (whatever his motives: she must have wondered!) would be able to help her. He was eager to record the erosion of her femininity – he was not interested in elderly female disfigurement. Hence the simple commercial transaction noted early in 1859: 'Took Mary Anne's shawl out of pawn & went with her to the photographer.'[6]

Munby visited Mary Bell again in 1860. She was sewing garments at home because her disfigurement prevented her from working with others. The visit was another occasion for Munby to ponder the subversion of femininity represented by Bell's noseless face: the comeliness of her body contrasting with her 'ruined face' and her 'hideous hole'. What a contrast with the ladies of his acquaintance:

… here is a girl of nineteen, whose utmost ambition, in the way of vanity, is to possess *a nose* – yet who is contented & happy without one: she would give much for that shapeless proboscis of which you, my dear, are so painfully conscious that it is not aquiline or Grecian.

As he watched her in the firelight, with the shadows awry for want of a nose, he thought that she looked like 'the ugliest of baboons'.[7]

My story has many beginnings because it involves several cultural histories: horror, fetishism, voyeurism, Victorian sexuality, fears of degeneration, ideals of femininity, concepts of the self. The subject is deceptively simple, a woman's nose, or rather a woman's missing nose – absent like the lost photograph. Yet I will argue that we can use this absent nose to detect – to sniff out – the cultural fissions of mid- to late nineteenth-century Europe. We will see that the cultural history detected by this nose is by no means simple narrative. In such multiplicity, there are many avenues of analysis to pursue, but in the interests of clarity I will focus on male constructions and deconstructions of femininity.

When Munby died in 1910, an acquaintance spoke of his sympathy for people 'who had to work for their living': '[W]hen walking along the lanes he would, if he saw a working girl, stop and speak words of good cheer to her.' The man told the *Daily Mirror* that Munby 'was really a most charming man, and his one idea seemed to be to make people happy'.[8] This makes our subject seem much more innocuous than he was, for there was a darker side to Munby that has barely been touched on by his biographer and historians. He collected noseless women. This story has never been told before.[9]

II

Munby encountered many noseless women.[10] But there was one woman who figured more prominently in his journals than any of the other noseless ones. Munby met Harriet Langdon in Ilfracombe in 1861, during a visit to Peter Roget (of *Thesaurus* fame). The experienced voyeur saw a heavily veiled woman – 'erect and elegant' like a lady – and knew from the hang of the cloth that it concealed 'ruin'. Without hesitation, he approached her and asked if he could see her face. The woman obliged, revealing a face ravaged by lupus. It was, recorded Munby, 'one of the most hideous faces I ever saw': noseless, with rotting lips and sunken eyes. 'Scarce to be called a face', it was 'ghastly as a skull'. Expertly, he inscribed the mental image of the tall elegant figure with the loathsome countenance, the contrast between the hidden horror and the dainty bonnet and soft brown hair which provided its feminine frame – a woman clinging to 'any crumb of hope' offered by a total stranger who had seen her by chance and who might never see her again.[11]

However, he did return to see her. Thus began an association of voyeurism and dependence which lasted for many years. She was in her late twenties and had been afflicted for almost as many years. Her parents were dead, so she supported herself by taking in needlework. Munby mused how her deformities would have robbed her of a normal childhood and adolescence: 'no girlish gaiety ... no womanly companionship and love', '... how should she have a sweetheart, whom no man can look at without horror and disgust?'[12] He promised to inquire about medical help in London, gave her a shilling (which she accepted reluctantly) and then departed.

Munby arranged for Langdon to go to London in 1862, having gained her admission to the Free Hospital in Gray's Inn Road. He met her train at Paddington Station and travelled with her on an omnibus. She wore a thick black veil, which, although it hid the actual ravages of her features, served as an obvious signifier of the horrors that lurked within. When they were walking down from Kings Cross to the hospital, Munby got her to lift the veil to show him her face: '... poor creature, it was more hideous than ever.' He recorded the reaction of the surgeon when he examined her: 'I noticed a little spasm of horror even on his calm professional countenance.' 'It was indeed much as if a skull had suddenly revealed itself in lieu of a woman's face.' After Langdon had been admitted, the doctor told Munby that it was the worst case of lupus that he had seen. The relevant diary entry finishes with Munby's self-congratulation on gaining the trust of 'a young and lonely woman' – it exudes the sense of power that he gained from such relationships.[13]

There were other occasions for Munby to record Langdon's hideousness and gratitude. He went to see her in hospital. The red firelight played upon her noseless face as he relayed the doctor's prognosis: she would not be able to have a false nose, but a mask was a possibility. 'God bless you Sir!' she said.[14] He made inquiries about a mask and placed an advertisement in the *Telegraph* in an attempt to get her a position.[15] He took her to her sister's home at Brompton when she was discharged from hospital. When they reached their destination, Munby got her to lift her veil so that he could inspect her face. It was, he wrote later in his journal, 'as ghastly and hideous as ever'. Her missing nose and distorted mouth made 'the smile of this young woman look like the grinning of a skull'.[16] It is clear that Munby expected to be able to look at Langdon's face whenever he wanted to. Once, when Langdon came to him for her monthly allowance, Munby asked her to pause before she lifted her veil so that he could prepare himself for the 'fearful revelation'.[17] As with Hannah Cullwick (his servant wife), the relationship involved the woman's self-abasement. Munby's diary contains Langdon's ritualized admissions to her ugliness and noselessness: 'And why, indeed, do I care for you? "Because" answers the poor girl, looking down, "Because I am ugly; because I am your *noseless sister*!"'[18] 'I have no nose – my nose is gone.'[19]

Munby arranged for Langdon to be photographed on numerous occasions, recording the shocked reactions of the photographers.

(When Munby collected the photographs, one man said '... what a "dreadful object" ... and asked if she could not be cured?' Munby told him that she had been cured.)[20] One operator was too horrified to take the picture and had to get another to do it. Again, Munby took curious satisfaction in the photographer's reaction: '... her face *is* exactly like a Death's head!'[21] Munby's journal also contains descriptions of Langdon looking at her own likeness – 'the dreadful portrait of her'. The disfigured face looks at the disfigured face: 'It makes your face look much more hideous than it is', said Munby.[22] All of these photographs have vanished from his archive.

The themes of Harriet's deformity are repetitious: the tragedy of the contrast between her 'comely' body and the face 'like a living skull'; her 'blank baboon like face'; her erased face and humanity. On outward show, Langdon was 'a beauty' with a nice dress, pretty bonnet and 'tall elegant figure'. Her thick veil hid the truth: 'a mere black blank within'. A literal lifting of the veil provided the contrast that so fascinated Munby.[23] 'Strange horror', he wrote in 1866 after many meetings, 'a tall elegant figure of a girl (she looks one, though she is 30) with hair & dress quite *à la mode*; and the profile of the face is simply a straight line, from forehead to chin.'[24] Elsewhere, he referred to the 'cruel irony in that contrast'. Langdon was a 'featureless sylph', a 'graceful monster'.[25] Compulsively, Munby charted the erasion of beauty that noseless women represented.

It is easy to see why historians have shied away from Munby's descriptions of noseless women. They make for disturbing reading, and it is impossible not to be repelled by Munby's behaviour. And yet these stories provide a unique entry into Victorian cultural worlds. Munby wrote candidly of his fascination with the mix of pity and repulsion he felt in the presence of Harriet Langdon: the 'horror' and 'strange emotion' he sought out and chronicled, 'the fascination of pity & the pathos of seeing a graceful feminine creature cursed with such a monstrous visage'.[26] Readers of his journals (and of this chapter) can experience their own blend of repulsion and fascination. The interest – for this writer at least – lies in trying to unravel the meanings represented by an absent nose.

III

Voyeurism was an obvious element in the interactions between Munby and 'his' women. As we have seen, he is often referred to as a *flâneur*; he used the term himself in 1863, noting that he forgot himself 'in the light studies of the flaneur – if a flaneur can be supposed to care about milkwomen, or about the comparative coarseness of servant maids' hands'.[27] However, if the *flâneur* is a silent observer of the city, this term will hardly do for Munby. He was no mute spectator, maintaining distance and anonymity. He was no ordinary voyeur.[28]

We can see this most clearly in his dealings with Harriet Langdon. Their visits to the photographer were always performative, involving layers of watching – Munby actually referred to exposing Harriet to the 'gaze of a stranger'. A visit in 1867 entailed a kind of macabre striptease – a literal unveiling. Langdon wore her veil, but underneath it was a false nose and lip. From the outside, she looked normal, potentially beautiful (with her graceful figure and a rose in her hair). She removed her veil to reveal 'a face that was not unlike a woman's'. But then, '… the time came for her to reveal herself in all her horror.' The amazed photographer looked on – 'scared and awestruck' – as she commenced her final unveiling and 'tore off her features'. Then began the last part of the performance, the visual capture of the image as Langdon was photographed in a variety of poses: 'It was worst when he took her with her shawl around her face: a death's head in a black frame, & still the dress and hands of a living tender girl below.' 'A young woman, graceful in figure, & tasteful: and yet, instead of being charming & attractive, the sight of her is so loathsome that her very picture must be kept apart from all others.'[29] I just referred to the last part of the performance, yet the true finale occurred two weeks later, when Langdon visited Munby and looked at the photographs, commenting on her stolen beauty.[30]

Munby's voyeurism was unrelenting:

One can fancy it: a tall young woman, thickly veiled, but attractive in figure and neat in dress, is shown into the old gentleman's sitting room: she curtsies, gives her name, but keeps her veils – for she wears two or three – close drawn: he bids her sit down, & after a while asks – perhaps with some misgiving – to see her face.

Then she, knowing that it must out, lifts up the folds of crape and shows him – that she has no face! She looks down, meanwhile, so as not to see how *he* looks on first beholding her: she nervously twitches the handkerchief with which long habit has taught her to hide her ugliness when anyone approaches.

He, restraining his horror, says to her merely that he had no idea it was so bad: he sees at once that to bring her into human companionship is hopeless.

We can see the layers of watching at work here. Harriet Langdon provided the narrative which enabled Munby – as he watched her – to imagine the encounter. He watched the man watch Harriet. He watched Harriet *avoiding* watching the man because she could not bear to see the horror on his face: she was unable to return his gaze. Munby watched the lifting of the (multiple) veils to reveal not beauty but monstrosity – the erasure of a woman's face. The diary enabled Munby to watch it all over again, whenever he wished, and to recall the drama and context of the watching; how after her account of the meeting with the gentleman, she was reduced to tears because of her sister's unfeeling attitude, and how she sat in front of the window with the light playing upon what should have been a face. 'Her nose, if she had one, would have been caught by it too: but as it was, there seemed to be nothing, below her forehead, but a blank cavernous shade.' Munby made a sketch of her obliterated profile (illus. 21): the absent nose, the erased signifiers of character and womanhood.[31]

Whether she visited him or he travelled to see her, Munby was able to stage the contrasts that he desired. Thus in 1866, he described the view of Langdon from behind as she wrote at his table, a 'graceful figure' with 'soft ladylike hair': '... she turns round, and instead of the face you expect, there is a noseless apelike visage of inexpressible hideousness.'[32]

On one occasion, Munby took Langdon to the Academy to see the portraits on display and watched her watching. He was clearly aware of the contrasts between the 'comely faces' of others at the exhibition,

21 Harriet Langdon, 1863: 'I made a sketch ... of so pitiable a transformation.'

the 'portraits of fair women', and Langdon's own disfigurement.[33] At another time, they went to Covent Garden for the opera. As always on such occasions, the stage was merely an adjunct to the real performance for Munby. He imagined lifting Langdon's veil to shock the audience: '... the knowledge of what it concealed made the fresh young faces around seem fairer, & her isolation more dreadful.'[34] When they went to Kew Gardens, it was a similar opportunity for descriptions of puzzled passers-by trying to penetrate the veil that hung in front of Langdon's face, and for reminders of Munby's self-satisfied knowingness of the concealed horror. It was yet another staging of subverted femininity: the 'young neat graceful figure' and incongruous feminine vanity offset by the fact that she 'had *no face*'. Whenever they were in an isolated place, Munby encouraged Langdon to remove her veil.[35] They also went to a circus; Munby watched her reactions. With her veil, she looked normal; he described the girlish laughter which came from behind the shroud. But then, in an effort to see things more clearly, she lifted the veil, and he caught a glimpse of her 'Death's Head' face – 'the delusion was over.'[36]

In mid-1865, Munby bought Langdon a domino mask of the sort worn at masques.

She tried on the mask, smoothing her hair over the edges of it; and the effect was startling; it gave her for the first time *a human face*. Her young figure and her soft hair seemed for once to have features to match; a shapely nose, smooth cheeks, and eyeholes through which her own eyes looked brightly. One fancied for a moment that it *was* her own face: and then, to take off that fair mask and see the hideous noseless reality underneath – the huge blubber mouth full of distorted fangs, that only grins when it means to smile! 'The truth is, you *have* no face in this world', say I: 'No, only in the next', the poor creature replies. As she sat down to sign her name, between me and the window, nothing could be more strange and ghastly than her profile (or want of profile) bending over the paper: no nose – but a white reflected light on the glazed tight skin of that blank and featureless visage. 'I know I am very ugly', she said.[37]

They tried a more life-like mask a month or so later with similar results. It was the face of a 'pretty girl' with a 'fresh pink complexion'. Munby revelled in the fiction that it was Langdon's real face: the face that matched her body and hair. However, this again merely served to accentuate the disguised disfigurement: '... it only made the grinning death's head more horrible, when she did take off the mask.'[38]

The mask, then, merely served to heighten Munby's fetishized sense of contrast. As always, the encounter provided an opportunity for both voyeurism and malice: 'The truth is, you have no face ...' It was not enough to experience and record Langdon's disfigurement; the pathos of her condition, her own recognition of her hideousness, had to be captured again and again: 'I'm sensible how very hideous I am!'[39] Munby's voyeurism did not involve the feeling of detachment and disengagement normally associated with the term. His impulse was to control, possess, create. The photograph is particularly suited to fetishism. It is small, contained, immobile, able to be touched. It is an image of a 'real' object, frozen in time. In handling a photograph, the viewer can engage in the fantasy of contact with the 'reality' behind the likeness. And the viewer is in total control over the duration of the look.[40] As Anne McClintock has observed, the camera also offered Munby's voyeurism the 'heightened pleasure of technical mastery over women' and fuelled his fantasies of 'sadistic omnipotence'.[41] But his repertoire extended far beyond the easy fetishism of the photograph.

Munby once used the handle of a toothbrush to probe the hole in Langdon's face. He described how the handle sunk in to a depth of several inches, 'as if to the very centre of her head'.[42] They experimented with pink paper pasted over the hole where her nose had been, and with a cork from a wine bottle! Then Munby produced a cardboard false nose, 'an elegant feminine shaped nose', attached from her forehead by a string. Ironically, the flesh-coloured paper did not match the blotchiness of Langdon's face. And although it provided her with the profile of a woman, the attempt to achieve normality developed into farce. 'It does not look natural', she said, removing the false nose.[43] He then had a friend bring back two artificial noses from Paris. The problem was that the false nose, like the paper one, only accentuated her rotting teeth and discoloured face.[44] The pretty upturned nose highlighted the lost femininity. It was, Munby wrote cruelly, 'a strange oasis of healthy form and colour amidst a desert of disease and deformity'.[45] The false nose would become incorporated into Munby's fantasies of subverted femininity. A month later, he was describing the incongruity of a woman gumming on her false nose and adjusting it in front of that signifier of feminine beauty and vanity, the looking-glass: 'Conceive the grotesque horror.'[46]

IV

Munby's voyeurism was inextricably linked to the emotion of horror – the term recurs in his descriptions – and this horror, in turn (like voyeurism), depended on the sex of the object of his gaze. What he

22 Femininity erased:
'Can this foul horror be a
woman's face …?'

experienced was what he once described as a 'thrilling awfulness': 'pity,
concern, disgust – horror, & yet the fascination of the horror'.[47] Indeed,
it could be argued that our story is a horror story. It has the classical
ingredients: fear and repulsion, the blend of 'terror and disgust' essential to the genre. Moreover, Munby's monster was a 'fusion figure',
violating expected (normal) categories. An animal/human hybrid, a
living cadaver, Harriet Langdon represented a 'violation of nature'.[48]

The theme of stolen femininity is central to this aesthetic of
horror, and clearly detectable in the disturbing sketches that Munby
made. One such image (illus. 22) accompanies an unpublished poem:

Can this foul horror be a woman's face,
The face of one who should be fresh & fair?
Can a young soul have such a dwelling place,
Or be condemn'd such hideous mask to wear?

Shut out from love, from life, she dwells alone,
And hides herself, lest any eye should see
How utterly her features are undone,
How like its skull a living head can be!

O'er the black gulf that was once her nose
The red skin tightens, blotch'd with ghastly green;
And all her shapeless mouth is set with rows
Of huge black teeth, and awful gaps between.

No human grace is left with her, to win
Regard for one so loathsome & so vile:
Her dead lips writhe into a demon's grin
When she, poor outcast! strives to form a smile.[49]

Munby's skull-like sketches of Harriet Langdon (illus. 23, 24) represent the effacement of beauty, accentuated by the ladylike attributes of the rest of her appearance: slender neck, hair, and bodily profile and demeanour. If the viewer blocks off the disfigurement, the face and form appear to be that of a potentially attractive woman, but the disfigurement literally erases the qualities of feminine loveliness.[50]

Munby used Langdon's false nose to conjure up the image of the construction and destruction of femininity. She donned her wax nose to delude the willing viewer (for 'the desire to shape out a human aspect for a human being is so instinctive') that there, in the fading light, was 'a pretty girl – like a lady in a drawing room'. And, then, before Munby's eyes, she reversed the process:

'Yes, I will *take my nose off*!' she said, with a bitter laugh: meaning 'do not suppose I forget that I am only a poor disfigured creature after all'. And laying hold of it between her eyes, she began to denude herself of humanity. Never can *I* forget this process or the result. I saw the flesh of her face rise and quiver, as the glue slowly gave way: I saw this girl deliberately *tear off her nose & her upper lip*, till all was gone. And then she stood before me, changed in a moment from a fair young woman into a grinning noseless baboon. Her

23, 24 Sketches of Harriet Langdon, 1870.

lithe tall figure and elegant dress, her hair so bright and fashionably arranged, now only intensified the horror of this revelation, & made the frightful ugliness of her face more shocking by contrast with what she had just lost.[51]

The repeated imagery of masks and veils is significant. The veil recurs in eighteenth- and nineteenth-century literature; it can be found both in the Gothic novel and in fiction of the 1880s and '90s, including Rider Haggard's imperial romances.[52] In Matthew Lewis's popular and controversial Gothic novel *The Monk*, veils are continually slipping or being lifted. The 'Bleeding Nun', a female ghost, lifts her veil slowly to reveal

an animated Corse. Her countenance was long and haggard; Her cheeks and lips were bloodless; The paleness of death was spread over her features, and her eye-balls fixed steadfastly upon me were lustreless and hollow. I gazed upon the Spectre with horror too great to be described.[53]

As Eve Kosofsky Sedgwick has put it, the veil is suffused with sexual meaning: '…the veil that conceals and inhibits sexuality comes by the same gesture to represent it, both as a metonym of the thing covered and as a metaphor for the system of prohibitions by which sexual desire is enhanced and specified.'[54] The veil can conceal either savoured beauty or unpredicted horror. The frisson is most intense when the senses are tricked by surface appearances into the wrong anticipation. Munby's noseless women did not adhere to all of the Gothic conventions, but they provoked what Sedgwick has termed the Gothic aesthetic of 'pleasurable fear'.[55] The 'fascination of the horror' was compelling for Munby. Certainly, he wrote, '… the Pigfaced Lady, the Veiled Prophet, Monk Lewis's Female Satan, none of these could be more appalling than the loathsome metamorphosis of this young woman, who cannot remember what it is to have a human face.'[56]

Yet these languages of horror were not limited to polarities between death and beauty, deformity and perfection. The reader will also have detected a human/animal axis: Langdon's missing nose rendered her baboon-like. It was as if she degenerated before Munby's eyes, regressing in moments from a stage of feminine perfection to primitive animality.

The literary examples invoked so far have been of noseless men. However, there is a case of a noseless woman. She appeared in 1885 in Rider Haggard's *King Solomon's Mines*:

I observed the wizened, monkey-like figure creeping from the shadow of the hut. It crept on all fours, but when it reached the place where the king sat it rose upon its feet, and throwing the furry covering from its face, revealed a most extraordinary and weird countenance ... *There was no nose to speak of*, indeed the whole visage might have been taken for that of a sun-dried corpse, had it not been for a pair of large black eyes still full of fire and intelligence, which gleamed ... like jewels in a charnel-house.[57]

This character is closer to the figure of Harriet Langdon than the noseless men. Indeed, Haggard's novels contain repeated slippages between the feminine and the simian in a manner that has resonances with Munby's predilections. In *She* (1887), the beautiful Ayesha regresses, within minutes, to a hideous monkey: the monkey and the beautiful woman are the same being:

At last she lay still, or only feebly moving. She who, but two minutes before had gazed upon us the loveliest, noblest, most splendid woman the world has ever seen, she lay still before us, near the masses of her own dark hair, no larger than a big monkey, and hideous – ah, too hideous for words. And yet, think of this – at that very moment I thought of it – it was the *same* woman![58]

The Darwinian connection is clear. Charles Darwin slipped continually from discussions of the behavioural traits of Europeans to 'savages', and then to animals, in a hierarchical ordering of data.[59] Rebecca Stott has argued that the evolutionary metaphors in Haggard drew on a popular discourse that had absorbed – in acceptance or rejection – Darwinian notions linking humankind and the apes, and on scientific theories that saw women as positioned closer to savages and animals in the evolutionary hierarchy.[60] There was thus an anxiety about the fragility of the barrier between human and animal, and a fascination with the possibility of the existence of living 'missing links'.[61]

Harriet Langdon's ape-like image showed how narrow the margin was between human and animal. It signified erasure not just of femininity but also of humanity; it rendered her baboon-like. Munby noted that 'her likeness to an ape, in spite of her neat dress & her chignon, made one shudder ... A chimpanzee with human figure & eyes: an elegant bright-haired young woman with the face of a baboon!'[62] He referred to her eating her food like a beast, 'as an ape would'.[63] It was this slippage, revealed in the tortured countenance of a shapely young woman, which so horrified and fascinated our *flâneur*.

V

To understand the full implications of the erasure of Harriet Langdon's features, we need to turn to the belief in physiognomy so influential in the Victorian period. The author of 'Faces', a piece in *Household Words*, captured the logic behind Munby's reactions. The face was the 'outward index of the passions and sentiments within': 'Between the head of a Shakespeare or a Bacon, and that of a Newgate murderer, there is as much difference as between a stately palace standing apart and a rotting hovel in a blind alley.' It was believed that the 'spiritual principle writes its own character on its exterior walls'.[64] Physiognomy – whose remnants still exist in the terms *highbrow* and *lowbrow* – was commonplace in nineteenth-century artistic and literary culture, whether as a conscious scientific language and means of representation and classification, or as less self-conscious popular assumptions and discourse: Victorians simply did not read and see as we do.[65] The body – particularly the face and head – was a guide to temperament and character. As one physiognomist expressed it, '... all human beings carry charts of their mentality and character at their mast-heads, legible, even in detail, by all who know how to read them.'[66] Physiognomy readily reflected Victorian attitudes to race and class, and, with its ease of classification, gave added power to warped representations of what were seen as natural hierarchies. Thus the Caucasian was the favoured type (indicated by skull shape and facial profile), and the Negro and other racial types were placed in the lower ranks of civilization and physical development, shading, disturbingly, into animality (the ape). Physiognomy proclaimed class in an analogous manner: there were distinct upper- and lower-class types, the latter lining up with the savage and the animalistic.[67] As a late nineteenth-century commentator put it, '... the forehead, eyes, and orbits are not relatively so large and developed; also the bridge of the nose is more often sunken; the chin is more often receding; and the lower part of the forehead less prominent in the lower, than in the better cultivated classes.'[68]

Within these broader categories were more specific classifications of character. Thus the forehead, eyes, nose, mouth and ears were individually invested with hidden meaning. The nose – the central part of the face, the determiner of profile – was seen as especially significant. The aquiline profile – the so-called Grecian nose – was favoured (illus. 25). There are particularly obnoxious profiles in the physiognomical texts (illus. 26), ranking, in descending order, Apollo, 'a negro' and a young chimpanzee.[69] A high and prominent nose demonstrated 'aestheticalness' (appreciation of beauty), visualized in

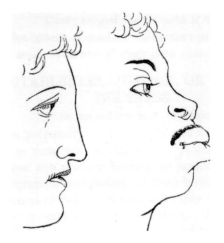

25 Contrasting profiles: 'Apollo, the Grecian classical ideal of the highest civilization, contrasted with ... the negro face' (J. S. Grimes, *The Mysteries of the Head and the Heart Explained* [1875]).

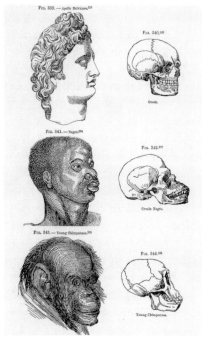

26 Hierarchies of civilization, descending physiognomies (J. C. Nott and G. R. Gliddon, *Types of Mankind* [1854]).

Joseph Simms's *Nature's Revelations of Character* (1879) in crudely contrasting illustrations of Charlemagne (aestheticalness large) and 'Kettle', 'a selfish and cunning Indian Chief' (aestheticalness small).[70] Snub noses suggested inferiority – though diminutive noses were more acceptable in women. A well-defined and prominent nose showed that its owner enjoyed great powers of reason. 'No person has been ever known as an original and correct reasoner', wrote the racist Simms, 'who had a low flat nose like that of the Chinamen.'[71]

Nasology, the classification of character according to nasal form, was a sub-branch of physiognomy. *Note on Noses*, a manifesto of nasology, established six classes of nose: the Roman (or aquiline); the Greek (or straight); the cogitative (wide-nostrilled); the Jewish (or 'hawk'); the snub; and the celestial (or turned-up). Each class was illustrated and characterized, with the Roman indicating decisiveness, energy and firmness, and the celestial and snub being sure signs of weakness and insolence. These categories were considered ideal types, and it was recognized that there would be hybrids that could be similarly classified. The ideal was a combination of the Roman, Greek and cogitative – 'the highest and most beautiful form which the organ can assume'.[72]

So, in his preoccupation with absent noses, Munby was merely engaged in a more fetishistic pursuit of common cultural markers. He was not working against the grain of his society. Like Munby, contemporaries read faces for their owners' class and character. Paintings were criticized when their subjects' physiognomy did not adhere to the facial or bodily code expected. Indeed, a more rigid code was expected of visual representation, wherein contradictions and anomalies could be erased by the artist's brush. Mary Cowling has shown the detail of fine aristocratic noses (and hands) in Frith's *Derby Day* (illus. 27): 'Their faces are long, their profiles straight, their noses aquiline, finely modelled with pronounced bridges, chiselled tips and well curved nostrils. The chins also conform to the current ideal: well founded but firm.'[73] Conversely, W. M. Rossetti (one of Munby's friends) was critical of Frith's *Railway Station* (1862) because the upper-class bridegroom in the painting did not have sufficiently refined features.[74]

Harriet Langdon had several artificial noses. One that Munby had bought for her was larger than the others, a 'masculine' aquiline nose. And so we get the further ambiguity of a masculine nose on a feminine face.[75] Langdon complained that the masculine nose was not as pretty as her feminine one: '… it doesn't suit my face; it's *not like me*; it's a *man's* nose.'[76] Noses, then, were also gendered. Indeed, the bulk of *Notes on Noses* is an unstated analysis of male noses: as with the one-sex model of pre-modern anatomy, where that one sex was male, the nose in this nasological text was a masculine, or unmasculine, nose.[77] It is only in the eighth chapter, entitled 'Of feminine noses', that it transpires that there were different classifications and rules for women: 'The subject of Nasology would not be complete without some observations on the Feminine Nose, because sex modifies the indications, some of which, though disagreeable and repulsive in a man, are rather pleasing, fascinating, and bewitching in a woman.'[78]

27 Aristocratic profiles: detail from Frith, *Derby Day*.

Thus the Roman nose, a positive attribute in a man, marred a woman's beauty (illus. 28, 29): it imparted 'a hardness and masculine energy to the face which is unpleasing, because opposed to our ideas of a woman's softness and gentle temperament'.[79] The celestial nose was desirable in a woman but abhorrent in a man: 'Weakness in a woman – which is gentleness, feminancy – is excusable and rather loveable; while in a man it is detestable.' 'A woman's weakness, too, is rather flattering, as it attests our supremacy.'[80]

Notes on Noses is a double manifesto, setting out the laws of classification while enjoining women to keep to their separate sphere. Classifications varied according to sex, but even where ideals coincided, the characteristics associated with the appropriate classification were explained in a highly gendered way. Thus the Greek nose, the most beautiful form of nose in women, was beautiful because it 'will not carry them out of their natural sphere': 'In the minor and domestic departments of life, where woman's influence is so peculiarly blessed, the refinements of the Greek Nose will appear in those household arrangements which make home the happiest and most beloved spot on earth' – that is, in needlework, the arrangement of furniture, interior decoration, the woman's own attire and so on. Whereas the male Roman nose anticipates action in the 'bustle and turmoil of the world', the female Roman nose should prefigure no such 'energy in the active departments of life', but rather energetic application to household matters, 'firmness and regularity in those duties which legitimately fall to her lot'.[81]

Moreover, it transpires that the absence of the female nose is far from incidental. Quite simply, the absent nose reflects woman's

28, 29 Masculine nose on a feminine face: 'Why, Dorothy had a sweet pretty little nose, and you –! Oh, my! Isn't it *tremendous!*' (M. A. Hoyer, *The Little Girl Who Did Not Like Her Nose* [1902]).

'happy inferiority'. The energies and tastes of women are weaker than those of men. Their passions are stronger, but passion is not constitutive of character:

> Whatever the cause, it is almost indisputable that women's characters are generally less developed than those of men; and this fact accurately accords with the usual development of their Noses. But for a small *hiatus* in the prosody, Pope's line would read equally well thus:–
>
> 'Most women have no Noses at all.'

Not, of course, that the nasal appendage is wanting, any more than Pope intended by the original line that women's characteristics were wholly negative; but that, like their characters, their Noses are, for the most part, cast in a smaller and less developed mould than the Nose masculine.[82]

The nose reinforced Victorian ideals of gendered femininity.

30 'Beauty, beauty with expression, and beauty with expression and intellect' (T. Woolnoth, *The Study of the Human Face* [1865]).

Victorian ideals of feminine beauty were mirrored in the literature of physiognomy. Robyn Cooper has shown in her discussion of Victorian beauty books that feminine charm was portrayed in terms of what distinguished woman from man: 'She is small, weak, soft, rounded, delicate.' Women had 'beauty and grace'; men possessed 'force and grandeur'.[83] Whiteness, fragility, refinement and delicacy were the key words for feminine attractiveness. Witness the illustrations of facial ideals in Thomas Woolnoth's *The Study of the Human Face* (1865), where male 'Resolution' (firmness, determination, 'character') contrasts with feminine 'Beauty'. True, the illustrations of feminine beauty (illus. 30) give three choices: abstract beauty, beauty with expression and beauty with expression and intellect. They do allow for the attractive qualities of female intelligence. But abstract beauty is also desirable – with its look of 'a pleasing void'. What distinguished female loveliness from plainness was an oval face, arched eyebrows, round eyes, undulating lips and ... a straight nose.[84]

In terms of physiognomy, then, Harriet Langdon was doubly deformed. It was impossible to read her character, for its outward façade had been erased. The disfigurement of her face had clouded what Simms would have described as her 'facial mirror'.[85] The inward soul was opaque, unreadable:

The face being the symbol of the soul, there is a pathetic and (so to speak) repulsive fascination in looking on a marred or obliterated face like hers, with the soul fresh & unchanged behind it: a coin that has lost its image, and who shall now say what its image is?[86]

The other loss – the main deformation for Munby – was Harriet's femininity. As he observed, '... this Satanic skull is the countenance of a gentle honest young woman!'[87] Beauty, and lost beauty, were obvious themes in the literary examples discussed earlier. As Darwin once observed, of all the parts of the body, '... the face is most considered and regarded, as is natural from its being the chief seat of expression and the source of the voice. It is also the chief seat of beauty and of ugliness, and throughout the world is the most ornamented.'[88] Indeed, Sander L. Gilman has demonstrated the centrality of the nose (so to speak) in the cultural history of aesthetic surgery.[89] Yet Harriet Langdon had no nose at all.

VI

It is important to remind ourselves that we are dealing with absent rather than ill-shapen noses. The origins of rhinoplasty lie not just in nineteenth- and early twentieth-century attempts to transform/mask the perceived deformities of race (signified by the all-too-present nose of 'the Jew'), but with efforts to reconstruct the ravages of sex (signified by the missing nose of the syphilitic).[90] Gilman has argued persuasively that the absent (or tiny) nose was linked to sexual degradation in *fin-de-siècle* Europe. Venereal disease could lead to the loss of the nose; thus facial features were a visible badge of dissolute behaviour and moral decay. Hence the dreadfulness of yet another noseless literary figure, Erik, the 'Phantom of the Opera' in Gaston Leroux's novel of 1910.[91] As Gilman has argued, Erik was intended as an object of erotic dread. With his death's-head face, rotting flesh and pursuit of the beautiful singer Christine Daae, he was the personification of sexual pollution.[92]

We have seen little evidence for overt sexual links in Munby's descriptions of 'his' noseless women, and it is tempting to argue that Gilman's observations about nasal deformity as a marker of sexual degradation did not apply here.[93] However, there are suggestions of a subtext in Munby's discourse. When he visited Gray's Inn Road Hospital to consult a surgeon about a mask for a particular noseless woman, he saw that the floor above contained the prostitutes' ward. The porter told him that some of these women had been facially disfigured because of venereal disease. The surgeon's nasal skills were presumably a result of his work with the ravages of syphilis.[94] Even though there was never any explicit mention of an association between sexual excess and disfigurement in the women with whom Munby had dealings – indeed, the circumstances of their loss were always given as non-venereal – there may well have been a sexual subtext in the representation of their disfigurement and in the reactions of those who saw them. Indeed, a prominent German facial surgeon observed in 1834 that noselessness was generally read as a punishment of sin: 'No one ever asks whether the nose was lost because a beam fell on it, or whether it was destroyed by scrofula or syphilis.'[95] Lupus, the ailment that afflicted Harriet Langdon, was known to produce identical ravages to syphilis.[96] Munby's sketches of her bear remarkable resemblance to an eighteenth-century engraving of the head of a syphilitic prostitute, 'the hidden face of the polluted female',[97] and to a nineteenth-century image of syphilis/death disguised as a beautiful young woman (illus. 31). Moreover, hereditary syphilis, part of the medical panoply of degeneration, surfaced in the 'simian' look, the cue to a reversion to bestiality.[98]

In a sense, we should not be too surprised by what we have encountered in these stories. The association between death and female beauty was a nineteenth-century commonplace.[99] Nina Auerbach has

31 Syphilis: 'A young suitor kneels before Death disguised as a lovely young girl' (A. M. Barthélemy, *Syphilis* [1851]).

observed that 'Victorian culture abounds in icons of beautiful corpse-like women' – what Bram Dijkstra has termed a tendency towards 'a necrophiliac preoccupation with the erotic potential of woman when in a state of virtually guaranteed passivity'.[100] But Langdon's visage was far from Rossetti's *Beata Beatrix* (*c.* 1860–70) or Millais' *Ophelia* (1851–2). It is not even comparable to the beautiful female cadavers of nineteenth-century anatomist art, awaiting their unveiling by dissection.[101] It was a skull, a *memento mori*, whose ultimate horror lay in the fact that the death's head was *living*, not dead or merely pictorial. As Christine Daae observed when she compared the Phantom's visage to that of the truly dead, '... *their* dumb horror was not alive'.[102]

The story I have told is a tale of horror. Harriet Langdon was a Victorian 'monstrous feminine'.[103] She represented what has been termed the abject, the 'place where meaning collapses'.[104] Her living body signified multiple crossings: into death, animality and the annihilation of beauty. Kelly Hurley has recently explored what she has usefully called the 'abhuman' figure of *fin-de-siècle* Gothic fiction, the 'not quite human subject', a product of the anxieties provoked by degeneration theory and pre-Freudian psychology.[105] Munby's phantoms were earlier manifestations of very similar cultural apprehensions. In the case of the noseless women, it was femininity that was so terribly marred by the mask of death. Conventions of the feminine – posture, a shapely body, attractive hair and clothes – framed this mask of death and disfigurement to make even more telling the horror of the essential femininity effaced and trapped within. My claim is that for Munby, these de-formations served, powerfully, to confirm their opposite: the feminine ideal. The very appeal of such subversions was the strengthening of their 'other'.

It is worth finishing by comparing Munby's sketch of Harriet Langdon with a strikingly similar image of a female skull in *Death Head Triptych*, a work by the modern performance artist Orlan, whose art includes surgery on her own body.[106] Munby's is a representation of stolen femininity; Orlan's is part of her quest to subvert modern idealized notions of female beauty. My theme has been the reinforcement of certain Victorian ideals through the representation of their 'other'. But I am far from claiming any fixity of interpretation. Monsters, in Judith Halberstam's telling phrase, are 'meaning machines', capable of both disciplining and disrupting.[107] Indeed, Munby recognized the underlying power of his 'creation' and – exasperated by her 'demands', unhappiness and ingratitude – described the poor woman as 'a kind of Frankenstein monster'.[108] This loaded description echoed identical fears in his relationship with Hannah

Cullwick: the sense of power of creating and manipulating, combined with an equally compelling terror that the experiment would get out of control. That is why he worked so assiduously to contain his demons.

Orlan's next project, by the way, is to construct a new nose: 'a very large nose – the largest nose technically possible'.[109]

3 Venus in Dirt: Servitude and Mastery

I

Ann Morgan's Love (1896) is a long-forgotten work by a minor Victorian poet about a servant, 'Bare-arm'd and buxom, rosy with her toil', who marries her employer.[1] He tries to tutor her in the ways of the gentry:

> For, he would show them what a woman is,
> Simply as woman: how she can be raised,
> By virtue of her very womanhood,
> From lower levels ...[2]

The experiment fails, and it is decided that she will return to the country. The master retires and lives with his wife in cottage simplicity. The poem contains descriptions of the everyday labours of rural life and idealization of the female labouring physique. The poet's ideal of womanhood is nobility achieved through hard work and service. He had, as one critic expressed it, a 'rather exaggerated view of the attractiveness of the most menial type of service'.[3] The literary reviewers responded predictably:

No man who knows women will have failed to see many who have delighted in the washing and dressing of children, in the happy work of gardening and tending of flowers, and even in the arranging of the table and in the homeliest work of the needle and the laundry.

'A man who has to go beneath his own natural level of taste and culture to find the true homeliness of a woman's nature', the *Listener* reviewer continued, must

be either a singularly unfortunate or a singularly unobservant man; nor can we see what advantages the labour of scrubbing and cooking and gathering up manure for the garden, which [the poet's] hero so much admires in his wife, has over the tending of children, the plain needlework of the fireside, and the care of the garden, which come so naturally to the most delicate and refined women in all spheres of life.[4]

Although the poet was fascinated by disruptions of stereotypes of upper- and middle-class femininity (an obsession with hands permeates his verse), womanhood remains strongly gendered: 'Your big red arms and your tremendous hands, / Are feminine.'[5] Ann Morgan is gentle, 'comely', with an 'innocent mouth' and 'soft red lips'.[6] She blushes and grows pale beneath her black face and ruddy hands. She swoons. The assumption of her creator seems to have been that a rough exterior, made hard through honest labour, hid a womanly interior. Her 'nature, rugged though it be / Is noble, and her maiden heart is pure'. Above all, she 'has the woman's gift, self-sacrifice'.[7]

This poet was also responsible for other verse involving upper- and lower-class romance and a mismatched relationship. *Susan* (1893) represented his feminine ideal:

> And what a queen of womanhood, was there!
> Tall and robust; by labour bronzed, yet fair;
> With large blue eyes, and soft abundant hair
> Hid by her housemaid's cap, whose snowy white
> Made all her rosy blushes glow more bright;
> Robust and tall, yet lissom and refined
> In shape, her large limbs suited well the mind
> That spoke expressive in her noble face.
> No servile soul was there; no kitchen grace
> Inspired her movements: she was one of those
> Who in the lowliest station never lose
> Their primal sense of woman's dignity.[8]

This strange hybrid also blushes under her dirt: 'Like a red sunset 'neath a thunder-cloud'.[9] She is outwardly a 'negress and a slave', but inwardly a 'Goddess'.[10] She is wife and servant at the same time.[11] This poetic manipulator is 'the new Pygmalion' with a 'woman form'd and fashion'd to his mind'.[12]

The reader will have guessed by now that this minor poet was none other than Arthur Munby. Although Munby wrote of the power of ennobling love, it was a very partial devotion. Woman's love was expressed through hard work and sacrifice; investing scrubbing with romance was how he once described it.[13] Ann Morgan demonstrates her love through drudgery, by labouring in, indeed beyond, her calling:

> That she was one of God's experiments,
> Which do not fail; a creature of His own,
> Not understood in an age like ours,
> And to our future, quite incredible.
> Yet, I do think she did not live in vain,
> Since one man understood her: and perhaps
> They who describe a nature such as hers

32 Creating the perfect woman: Edward Burne-Jones, *Pygmalion and the Image: II: The Hand Refrains*, 1875–8.

> Straight from the living soul, should first have known
> How women, freed by lowliness of birth
> From the quaint trammels of society,
> May use the very basest of their toil
> As sacraments of Love; and thus at length
> Ennoble all their passion and themselves
> To heights beyond the reach of ladyhood.[14]

Apart from some significant departures from the real-life script, *Ann Morgan's Love* is essentially the story of Hannah Cullwick, Munby's real-life servant/wife. '*I* am Ann Morgan,' Cullwick wrote, after she had seen the proofs of the book.[15] In 1893, they both read a review of *Susan* which claimed that a creature like her was an impossibility, and called her creator 'her Frankenstein'.[16] Both Frankenstein and his monster were amused by the irony of the situation: "'Why, it seems as he dunna think there *can* be a woman like me!' 'Yes, dear, and yet, there you sit, with your rough hands and in your servant's dress, before me!'"[17]

Among the paintings of Edward Burne-Jones are four oils derived from a series of sketches to illustrate William Morris's poems *The Earthly Paradise* (1870). These paintings, known as the Pygmalion series, tell the story of Pygmalion, the sculptor in Ovid's *Metamorphoses*, who creates the image of the perfect woman. It was an image, as the preamble to one of Morris's poems expresses it, 'fairer than any that had been seen, and in the end came to love his own handiwork as though it had been alive: wherefore, praying to Venus for help, he obtained his end, for she made the image alive indeed, and a woman, and Pygmalion wedded her'. Galatea is the woman of Pygmalion's fantasies (illus. 32). The woman in Burne-Jones's paintings is indeed a classical beauty: fair-skinned, with a straight nose, oval eyes and small hands. Her creator, the sculptor, looks rather effeminate.[18] Munby also attempted to create the woman of his fantasies. He tried to fashion her through the pen, the photograph, elaborate stagings and his own imagination. He failed. His Galatea was made of living flesh, but she was more resistant than marble.

II

Munby quoted his associate John Ruskin in support of his experiment: '... the best labour is unpaid labour, and the best service is done for love.'[19] He was aware that outsiders would not understand his relationship with Cullwick or 'do justice to the passion of immortal love that burns in her – and in me'. It was 'sacrilege, to subject such a love to the light of common day'.[20] Munby's theory was that no matter how much Cullwick was physically degraded, her moral purity would shine through: 'The outward vulgarity is far more than redeemed by the nobleness within.'[21] Cullwick's purity was proclaimed through her degradation in pursuit of her allotted role in society and in devotion to her master/husband:[22]

The very baseness of her lot was a joy to her; the coarsest implements or incidents of her toil – the soot, the grime, the blacking, the scrubbing brush, the sloppail – became for her the emblems and the utterance of her love for the man who had shown that he could honour & respect one like her, because of her lot and not in spite of it; and that he valued a love so strangely expressed, because the expression was appropriate and sincere, and helped to show what the humblest servant could be and do, and how great is the power of love, in transmuting foulest things to noblest essence.[23]

Munby's philosophy was that 'Nothing is low or disgusting if it be done for love.' Since, as a lowly servant, Cullwick 'was bred to do low & disgusting things for hire', she had to find 'things even lower than those she did for hire' to demonstrate her love and devotion to her lover and chosen 'Master'.[24] As Munby wrote in 1862, '… we must create our Utopia out of the materials at hand.' 'She … is trying to realize the ideal I set before her: a base ideal, for it is that of her calling, which is of the basest.'[25] In 1863, on the occasion of Cullwick's 30th birthday, Munby said that he had originally planned to make a lady of her 'by the ordinary method of education'. This had not been possible, so the scheme became for her to achieve nobility through 'servile labour': 'Physical degradation was to be the channel, and even the source of spiritual beauty.' What 'religious women of old' had tried was to be the task of an English servant.[26]

Cullwick's noble and unselfish love revealed itself in her face: her hard labour 'shows itself indelibly in her hands'.[27] Their roughness was a sign of a devotion expressed through hard work; they were 'the hands that have wrought for me'.[28] Although Munby excised sections of his earlier diaries that dealt with Cullwick's subservience, a surviving passage from 1859 gives some notion of his mind at the time. He referred to her as a modern-day Patient Griselda, the archetypal submissive woman: 'If she had but more, or less, of intelligence & imagination, so as to be either a heroic woman or a devoted slave, she would be pretty near perfect.'[29] He referred to her 'selfsacrifice' and 'noble selfabasement', inconceivable to the 'fools of the middle classes'.[30]

Munby was convinced that Cullwick came of nobler stock than her lowly position indicated, that she had 'better blood than she knows of'.[31] She was the scullion with the face of a duchess.[32] Physiognomy was central to Munby's world view: Cullwick's face was 'highbred'.[33] He collected stories to support his contention. An old man had told Cullwick that her profile was evidence that she had 'better blood in you than you know of'.[34] She had met two gentlemen in a railway carriage who were struck by the contrast between her ladylike face and her working hands.[35] Lowes Dickinson, the portrait painter and founder of the Working Men's College, saw a photograph of Cullwick and said that she had a 'noble and beautiful face'.[36] Another artist said that her photograph was undoubtedly that of a lady.[37] Munby's friend Robert Borland said that Cullwick had the hands and arms of a rough working woman, but the face of a lady, 'and of a *ladylike* lady'.[38] Munby pursued the theme of the hidden lineage in his poetry. Susan (based on Cullwick) had hidden gentility:

> And she was drest as other servants are,
> White-capp'd, white-apron'd; and the cotton print
> That mask'd her queenly figure, gave no hint
> That she could be a lady in disguise.
> But yet, her rosy mouth and clear blue eyes
> Had more of purpose, nobler character,
> Than a mere peasant's: one might well infer
> That some august progenitor in her
> Had reappear'd; so delicate and fine
> Her features were, so proudly aquiline.[39]

Dorothy too, in an earlier, anonymously published poem, was a labouring woman with a secret aristocratic father.[40] Munby was not *really* transgressing social boundaries: his liaison with a servant was not with just any servant, but with one with hidden gentility – or at least that was the fantasy.

It was this contrast within the same person which held such immense appeal for Munby. Not only was Cullwick a foil for 'the velvet cheeked golden haired ideals of youth and … the intellectual beauties that manhood worships'. Not only was 'every rag on her back and every smear on her face … a symbol of love & self sacrifice'. Her body encapsulated the triumph of inner nobility over a degraded exterior.[41] As he concluded in 1862, in a particularly chilling section of his journal that described Cullwick's exhaustion, despair and ridicule by fellow servants because of her unkempt and dirty appearance ('"Everybody hates me!" she sobbed; "I'm so dirty and shabby!"'): 'What interest is there in these mean & loathsome details of a vulgar life? There is some, I think, even where the work is as mean as her work; but much, when you have the pathos of contrast between her and it; as in my Hannah's case.'[42] The antithesis between the noble interior and the degraded exterior was everything for Munby.

Cullwick was a living demonstration of the feminine 'other', a foil to notions of genteel femininity. She sat *on* the kitchen table, 'her long legs dangling one on each side of a corner … and the tips of her strong boots just touching the ground'.[43] She caught flies with her hand: 'I once killed 100 in 5 minutes, for a bet with my fellow servant.'[44] She participated enthusiastically in a pig-killing. She collected horse dung off the road and dug it into the garden, and cleaned out the cesspool 'with her own hands ... in view of her neighbours'. She swept the chimney, showering herself in soot. She dusted the furniture with her bare palms. She spoke dialect. She never used a looking-glass. Instead of a corset, she wore a 'belly-band' made out of men's corduroy breeches. A leather wrist strap was her only bracelet. She dressed like a servant, calling her husband 'Master', 'Massa' or 'Moosiri', never by his Christian name. She ate separately from him in the kitchen, at 'working folks' hours', with blackened face and arms, using her fingers, putting her knife in her mouth, licking her plate, talking with her mouth full and wiping it with her hand.[45] She sweated.[46] All quite unlike a lady.

Moreover, these contrasts existed in the same individual: 'The contrast is great indeed, between this queenly being [the Hannah able to disguise herself as a lady and accompany Munby on outings], and the homely robust ruddy Hannah who now lives and works as a mere peasant.'[47] She was, wrote Munby, a 'double creature': 'lady and servant' (illus. 33).[48]

When she was to pass as a lady on her rare trips away with her husband, Munby, aware that others would read Hannah's body, had to erase the markings of commonality. Her face and hands held the key. The hands which shovelled coal, and the fingers which were her tongs, were scrubbed clean; the black labour lines, so easy to read, had to be blurred. Gloves concealed the roughness, but ladies' gloves were too small, so Hannah had to wear Munby's. A veil was imperative to hide her sunburnt complexion – the sure sign of an outdoor life. Thus prepared, and provided she spoke as little as possible, Hannah was ready to 'enter the area of civilization and culture'.[49] Henry Higgins and Eliza Doolittle, George Bernard Shaw's far more celebrated Pygmalion and Galatea, seem prosaic beside Cullwick and Munby. In Shaw's *Pygmalion* (1912) a working-class London flower-seller is transformed into a duchess. Tampering with the otherness of class effects the metamorphosis: Eliza is washed, her old clothing is burned, and she is taught the piano. But the focus of this transformation is speech. Eliza is taught to talk like a lady: '... you have no idea how frightfully interesting it is to take a human being and change her into a quite different human being by creating a new speech for her. It's filling up the deepest gulf that separates class from class and soul from soul.'[50] Hannah Cullwick's passing – when she passed – had little to do with speech except, that is, for its absence. She was mute when she appeared publicly as a lady. Munby knew the importance of speech as a class marker (hence Cullwick's silence), but for him class

was written on the body in ways that totally escaped Shaw. Passing
was achieved by dress and physiognomy. Hence the use of veil and
gloves to obscure tell-tale bodily signs. Such things were not even
mentioned in the other *Pygmalion*. Munby's aim was not to transmute
one class into another, as in Shaw's rather one-dimensional creation,
but to form a new being, his Galatea: a hybrid lady/servant.

IV

Cullwick's famous 'diary', kept during the time of the couple's
prolonged courtship, was actually loose daily accounts of her work,
written at Munby's request and sent to him for collating and binding
(Cullwick seems to have done the actual stitching as part of her work
when she visited him). She did not enjoy writing up her labour at the
end of a hard day, and complained and resisted. Their correspondence is full of apologies and procrastination: 'Is it any wonder that I
should tire of writing the things I had to write about. Its late now &

my head feels too bewildered to write,' she wrote at 11:30 one Monday night in 1870.[51] 'Don't trouble about the diary Massa i'll do it in time if all's well.'[52]

Hannah's diaries, therefore, should not be read as a straightforward account of her life. They were part of Cullwick and Munby's 'experiment', central to their disciplining, sadomasochistic relationship. She chronicled the minutiae, drudgery and dirtiness of her labour because her lover wanted to hear about it. The diary was part of their drama. Thus the entry for a Monday in which she describes blacking her face and going out on the front steps at 8:00 a.m., a time when people would be passing by, to rub her face and lips against the door mat – a 'sign what I promised Master i'd do'.[53] This is not to deny her agency. She knew that Munby would read her entries and used this opportunity accordingly:

i go to Massa every Sunday, but its all work to be with him fore 5 & then i'm generally tired & can say very little to him – i do my work for Massa to[o] – have just a little petting & away at 9 & home by ten, & then Monday begins … All this sounds like complaining but i am not, cause it was my own doing to take this place, but it's no wonder I feel dull & low spirited often, & get tired o seeing so little of Massa when I love him so, & him me.[54]

She wrote – knowing that Munby would read it – that he was cross with her because she had not sent her diary entries, 'but it wasn't my own fault.'[55] The diary, she wrote in a more heated moment, 'was a great plague to me, having it to write over & over again – just the same things every day, cause nothing fresh happens hardly'.[56] Munby also complained about her unwillingness to chronicle the 'monstrous facts of her kitchen life'. He explained it by her unease with a pen; she preferred cleaning to writing about cleaning.[57]

Despite Munby's glosses, slavery for love is the most appropriate description of their relationship. Cullwick was Munby's wife, servant and slave. In 1876, he recorded that she had been a servant for 35 years, and a 'slave (soidisant) for 23'.[58] 'This is a slave's work, my dearest,' he said when she bathed him and rubbed him down one morning.[59] When she was a maid of all work, she had sewn a monogram, which she pinned above her bed: the sacred letters IHS in yellow silk on a black background. She told Munby that they represented more than *Jesus Hominum Salvator*: 'Them letters … stands for I, Hannah, Slave … and I Have Suffered.'[60] She signed some of her letters 'your own slave', 'your own loving drudge'.[61] Munby claimed that the word *slave*, which he did not like to 'frame', was hers.[62] And he was convinced that she derived pleasure from the role.[63]

So servitude was pivotal to their relationship. As Cullwick wrote in 1870, '... seventeen years i've bin your *slave* – in every sense of the word. i've trusted, loved & *served* you.'[64] In 1874, when they were living together in London, Munby recorded Cullwick's birthday in his journal: 26 May, 'her 33rd. year of servitude; for my wife is still a servant'.[65] Munby said of Cullwick's early servant career, 'Hannah felt no shame in being lent, like a horse or a dog, by her mistress to another lady, who meant to use her as a common drudge.'[66] He stressed her 'passion for drudgery':

Hannah loved drudgery not only for its own sake, but also as a means of self humiliation. She loved it too because her sweetheart honoured her for loving it, and admired her 'in her dirt' as much as in her Sunday best, and he liked her hard red hands better than any white ones. And she loved it because it helped to intensify the outward contrast between her and him, and thus to show emphatically that she would not be his equal.[67]

Even Cullwick's dreams were about servitude: 'I dreamt I was in service again, Massa, an' I was cleanin out the sink hole, & eh, it was moocky!'[68] '*I was born to serve*', she told Munby, 'But I couldna serve nor love a common man, like I do you!'[69]

She would lick boots, she said to remove the dirt and soften the leather for brushing, but it certainly became part of their private ritu-als of slavery and humiliation. In 1892, on their nineteenth wedding anniversary, Cullwick wanted to lick Munby's boots. He lied that he had not let her do it since they had been married:

'Eh, Massa, surely I have, though? Then it's high time as I licked 'em now!' And straightway, she threw herself on the floor at his feet. He took her by the shoulders, and raised her, and clasped her and kissed her black lips, in a sort of shuddering rapture of humility and thankfulness: that such a creature, so lowly and pure and devoted, should show her devotion thus. The seeming degradation of this act is itself a glory to her: and a shame to him, if he allowed it now, and if he did not show her all honour in return. Even her tongue was black, so fervently had she done this thing.[70]

They were both obviously troubled by the relationship. Munby had a dream where she licked his boots in front of a group of ladies. Cull-wick dreamt that a lady got on her knees and licked Munby's boots, and that she, in jealous competition, licked them all the more enthusi-astically.[71] Munby was obsessed with the number of boots Cullwick cleaned every year when she was in service – some thousand pairs – and he calculated that she had cleaned nearly 35,000 pairs in her 37 years of 'service for hire'.[72]

The washing of feet was also clearly linked to the master-servant/slave interaction. From the very initial stage of their courtship, Cullwick's washing of Munby's feet formed part of their almost ritualized interaction. Much later, in 1891, when Cullwick was reading aloud from the *Odyssey*, Munby observed that she was particularly interested in the scene where Eurycleia washed Ulysses's feet, 'for that was one of the first things that Hannah ever did for her sweetheart'.[73]

It may seem anachronistic to describe their relationship as sadomasochistic. But it is difficult to find any other way of describing an interaction so charged with power and desire. Munby certainly had a sadistic, controlling streak, which he demonstrated in other relationships and encounters. We can see this in his diary for 1860, where we move from his condescending description of Cullwick to the humiliation of a servant. After reflecting on Hannah's 'simple submissive life' and ignorance, he wrote:

> ... let me at least work out some of my theories upon this tender slave: let me be refreshed and comforted by a mother's love, and by that of one so different: let me look on this hardworking simplicity, this humble devotion, which finds its highest expression in the doings of a chimney sweep or a lapdog, and feel, undeservedly, what I always meant to prove – that the veriest drudge, such as she is, becomes heroic when she truly loves.[74]

Days later, beginning on the next page of the diary, he was at the Crystal Palace, examining and delighting in the coarseness of the hands of a total stranger, a servant ('strange & surely noble, in a girl of nineteen, this quiet acceptance of degradation'), and offering her nothing but 'Cruel, brutal words': '... you have made yourself coarse and ignorant.'[75]

Cullwick once referred to it being 'painfully delightful to suffer so much for love': 'What is it i've pledged myself to be to you – your slave? Well then, I must come to you if you send for me.'[76] In a remarkable few pages dated 1890, Munby outlined what he described as the 'signs' in their relationship; in effect the signs of Cullwick's subjection, culminating in the 'great sign of all' – the distancing singular is all-important – 'her marriage'.[77] The first of the signs was the boot. The boot was an obvious symbol of authority, but it was also linked to blackness and dirt. The eroticization is clear in the description of boot-cleaning that prompted Munby's reflections. Cullwick had her hand inside the boot, where the foot went, signifying both intimacy (even penetration) and dirtiness. She got blacking on her 'highbred aquiline nose' – marring beauty – and another streak 'disfigured her sweet lips'. Looking at Munby – the gaze is crucial to the dynamics – she deliberately licked some dirt (not polish: Munby's word is 'mire') off the boot. Munby then kissed her, 'black as her lips were'. The act does not just exist on its own, but releases a store of memories about dirt and degradation: Munby had recollections of Cullwick licking his foot in public, out in the street, in front of some stable hands. The next sign was the labourer's leather wrist-strap that she wore day and night until it disintegrated. It declared publicly that she was a 'servant of the lowest kind'. It complemented her large, rough hands and contrasted with her 'lady-like face' (illus. 34). Finally, there was the private sign of her slavery to Munby – the term *slavery* is theirs – the small steel chain and padlock that Cullwick wore round her neck, inside her frock, and for which her 'Master' held the only key.[78]

The fact that she was his servant and slave was an obvious indication of the allocation of power in the relationship. When she was younger, Cullwick used to kneel between Munby's knees to say her prayers, and she admitted in 1892 that until 'quite lately' (she was almost 60 years old) she had said 'Make me a good child.' She told Munby that she liked to say her prayers to him because it made her feel 'childlike'.[79] Yet much of the appeal that Cullwick held for Munby lay in her strength, the knowledge that she was more powerful than him. He sat on *her* lap: 'I sat with her in the twilight … seated, an hour together, feet up, upon her knees; for to the "gentle giantess", my 12 stone weight is nothing.'[80] To end a quarrel in 1893, Munby 'sat on her lap, as he used to do of old; and her strong arms went round him, and she grew quiet and tender, like herself'.[81] Cullwick told Munby that she was not afraid to be left alone with any man; '… no man is strong enough to do me harm against my will.'[82] She was stronger than him; she could have overpowered him if had she wanted to. Indeed, Munby's diaries suggest that this happened on at least one occasion: '… the tall strong woman clenched her fists, and seemed about to spring upon her husband, as once she did before,' he wrote after an argument in 1887.[83]

And, vice versa, she was attracted by his softness. The relationship was complex, therefore, and we should certainly not think of female passivity. Cullwick was not afraid to voice her discontent, as we know from her letters: '… every year that you live alone, I can see that it makes you more selfish.'[84] In a letter written the following day, she referred to him as a selfish old bachelor.[85] She said that she would not visit him 'till I know your mind, & whether you are master of yourself as well as of me'[86]: 'I know that i do more for you than I would for any other man in the world, & so i expect love, & a *little* consideration in return.'[87] '*Naughty* Massa', she wrote on 1 November 1870,

34 Hannah Cullwick, servant: Note the display of the hand and the wristband. Taken in Salop, 1872.

How could you let me leave you so cooly o' Thursday night, when you know it makes me so unhappy – just because I didn't like that bonnet … I think you was very selfish & unkind to me, you let me sit & sew & never spoke – I wash'd your feet, & rubb'd you & all, & then you was as cool as a cucumber & let me go home by myself, like a *dog*, as in ann, back to my work in service.[88]

But for all sorts of reasons, Munby saw himself as the ultimate controller. He was what he described as the 'anxious warden' of Hannah's soul.[89] A favourite position of intimacy was Cullwick on her knees before the seated Munby, her face looking upwards to his.[90]

Photography was an important component of their complex routine of mastery and submission. Take the description of the photographing of Cullwick in 1862; Munby's text allows an insight into the construction of these images not apparent from the objects themselves. The very process of photographing formed part of Cullwick's 'self-sacrifice' and 'degradation': '… to blacken herself from head to foot, and stand thus, almost nude, before even that phlegmatic little German, this was something, truly.' Munby described this as a record of her 'noblest guise – that of a chimney sweep' (illus. 35).

Another pose had her crouching on the ground at Munby's feet – 'I doing my best to look down upon her like a tyrant!' Munby has been excised from the surviving photograph; appropriately, all that remains of him is the tip of his boot (illus. 36). Then, Cullwick arranged her own pose, sitting on the floor clad only in her shift and petticoat, with a bare foot showing. She told him later that this was her pose before she went to bed, and when she was thinking of him.[91] So the photographs were much more than images of working women. When Munby went to collect them from the photographer the following week, the two men discussed Hannah's body – 'as an animal' – noting her 'fine legs', her 'fine face', 'the swell of her long throat' and her strong arms.[92]

They returned in 1863, one of many visits. Cullwick went in her wet and fouled clothing, and the photographer rubbed charcoal on her arms to make them blacker for the photograph and told her to wipe her face with her dirty apron. Munby stood by transfixed. It is clear from his diary description that the photographs produced during this session must have been charged with meaning. Here was the object of his love being degraded and disciplined (his words) in front of him, while she stood there without complaint.[93]

When Munby and Cullwick were first secretly married and lived
together, she as his servant rather than his wife, he derived voyeuristic
satisfaction from hearing about her interactions with other tenants in
the building:

Hannah had been waiting on my tenant Mr. Napier: and she heard him say to
someone '*the woman* told me' so & so, meaning herself: for *she* is 'the woman'
– the servant who waits on us all, and digs coals & draws water, and blacks
grates and lights fires and scrubs the floors and cleans the boots: she does all
this daily, as a matter of course, and in the humblest servant's dress.[94]

Thus he was able to record her fetching and carrying, her service for
his neighbours, with the secret knowledge that it is his wife, the wife
of their landlord, who was talked to in a condescending manner and
ordered about.[95]

'Thankyou, Sir', my Hannah meekly answered; she thanked this stranger for
giving her leave to sit down in her own parlour. 'But I only sat on the edge of
the chair', she told me, 'for of course I felt awkward, to sit down at all before
a gentleman; and I soon got up again, and stood before him, with my black
arms resting on my coarse striped apron, and my strap plain to see.'[96]

75

The descriptions appear as though Munby actually witnessed the scenes described, but he was not there. They are, one assumes, a mix of Cullwick's reportage and Munby's wishful thinking, questioning and crafting; we must allow for the possibility of the hidden interrogations and inventive shaping of text which lie behind the immediacy of the conversational prose. The voyeurism is heightened by Munby's technique of 'quoting' both the reported interaction and Cullwick's account of it: 'I only sat on the edge of the chair.' It is unlikely that interactions were remembered precisely. Would Cullwick really have said, 'I soon got up again, and stood before him, with my black arms resting on my coarse striped apron, and my strap plain to see'? However, the point is that living together widened the possibilities of the theatre of their interaction: the drama of master/servant could be played out on a wider stage. The passage above also includes a description of the tenant, Thornbury, examining Cullwick's muscular arm: '… she submitted, even as a slave might submit to be handled by her purchaser.' It ends (predictably) with Thornbury's attempt to kiss her, which she quietly rebuffed.[97] Years later, Munby recalled Cullwick telling him that she had crawled around on all fours, scouring and cleaning; he revelled in imagery of her trying on a gentleman's gold and diamond rings, too small for her swollen, blackened fingers; and he recounted his tenant Thornbury's attempts to kiss her.[98]

V

For John Ruskin, who taught with Munby at the Working Men's College, 'well-chosen reading' led to 'the possession of a power over the ill-guided and illiterate'. Reading was a means of raising those of a lesser 'moral' or 'thoughtful state'. Books (of the right kind) permitted access to the thoughts of 'the wisest and greatest men'.[99] Munby employed reading as a means of fashioning Cullwick. As he wrote in *Ann Morgan's Love*, she would be raised by education if not in the cultural refinements of class:

> … she did not rise
> In outward rank, in manners, nor in speech,
> Nor, least of all, in dress or finery;
> But of an evening, when she read to him
> And ask'd him questions, or he read to her
> And talk'd, his clear illuminating touch
> Lit up the volume, till her fallow mind

Received that nurture and retain'd it well.
So, step by step, in methods of his own,
He raised her; till she gain'd a breadth of view
That took in all he wish'd; and soon display'd
An active eager interest in mankind …
That made her a companion for himself
Beyond all other women.[100]

He liked to rule people with 'an intellectual empire', it was said of an Egyptian ruler in one of the books which Cullwick read aloud to Munby; "'Aye", said Hannah, looking up slyly, as she read it, "an that's how you like to rule *me!*"'[101]

Indeed, the simple act of reading aloud, still common practice in the nineteenth century, provides an excellent example of Munby's mastery. The act may have been unproblematic, but its meanings were complex. We know that Munby used the performance of reading as an occasion to celebrate the rural Englishness which he found so attractive and which he felt was personified in the figure of his 'peasant' bride. On one memorable occasion, something of a coup in terms of staging, he managed to get Cullwick to read Sidney's *Arcadia* after she had finished gleaning:

Her dinner was a gleaner's meal; a dish of hot bacon and beans, which she held on her knees as she ate it; while her mug of broth stood by, on the table. But when she had eaten it, and had wiped her mouth with the back of her hand, she did read Sidney; leaning back in her chair, in a highbred ladylike way, and reading as well as if she were a lady, and not a Shropshire gleaner.[102]

As the Sidney reference suggests, one of the main roles of reading for Munby was as a theatrical occasion for reminders of class and gender crossings. Books for Munby were symbols of status. He wrote once of the world of the drawing room with its books, piano and pictures as 'outside and above' the lives of the servants who lived below and cleaned and maintained drawing-room life. Servants were so near and yet so far from these material markers of civilized life.[103] When Hannah, the servant, picked up a book, these chasms were breached. Thus reading was much more than mere reading. In these fascinating stagings, bodies were being read as well as books. In the words of Cullwick herself, it was an occasion for the 'sudden transition from kitchen to parlour; from cookin as a servant to sittin down to read to you!'[104] She read and enjoyed Anne Thackeray's *Miss Angel* 'as thoroughly as any lady might'; she read with 'all the ease and grace of an educated person': 'Hannah read aloud with an archness and vivacity quite charming.' She read moving passages 'with emotion, with a broken voice'. Yet she held the white-paged book with a 'brown rugged hand' and was dressed like a peasant and servant.[105] As Munby explained,

... the contrast is strangely piquant, as she sits there before me, in her cotton frock and blue-check kitchen apron and large white servant's cap, the leather strap on her bare arm, and her shapely but rough and red-brown hands holding the book, whatever it be, from which she reads some of the grandest or most refined of human utterances with lively interest, and with a force and propriety which no lady could excel.[106]

The lines of print in the white-paged book formed a curious image next to the black labour-lines which criss-crossed Cullwick's hands, giving her skin 'an uniform tint of Indian ink'. But 'her black fingers left no stain on the white margins of the leaves, as she held the book, and read it like a lady.'[107]

'Do you know of any *lady* as 'ud read to yo, 'an get your dinner ready too?' Cullwick asked Munby one evening, after she had finished reading *Mary Barton*.[108] So the ritual of reading aloud was incorporated into the kaleidoscope of class contrast and contradiction that formed Munby's view of the world. It was one of the fragments in the mosaic, juxtaposed with the blackness of labouring life, and Cullwick was able to move effortlessly from one sphere to the other – from 'digging coals' to 'reading of Egyptian theology'.[109] One evening she asked what 'anomaly' meant. Munby explained that it meant something out of the usual course, something seeming out of place. '"Ah" says she, "then I'm an anomaly, sitting here in this room, and reading to you!"'[110]

Reading was the site where Cullwick's two natures were declared: her peasant side – 'rude, homely, frugal, hardworking', 'uncouth', 'most picturesque' – and her 'lady's nature' – 'refined, highly emotional, capable of taking an interest in the loftiest subjects and of reading about them'.[111] These two natures were reflected in Cullwick's body, indeed in the parts of her body most displayed when reading: the face, mouthing the words and expressing emotion, and the hands which held the book. Munby claimed to read her body as she read her book. Her face held the key to her 'lady's nature', the physiognomy of the gentility which Munby was convinced lay in her ancestry. Her hands declared both her peasant's nature and the potentiality of lady-hood: '... the outward and visible sign of her calling, are symbols of her double nature.' 'They were once so hard, that she used to slice the horn off her palms and fingers, and send it to her sweet heart, as a token of love and labour.' They were, as Cullwick said, a testimonial to her hard work – 'a character to me' – and she would hold them out so that potential employers could read this fleshly testimonial to hard labour. 'Yet her hands, though marred by life-long labour, are shapely; the fingers & nails show a fine race; and a few weeks of idlenesse would again make her hands ladylike and soft.'[112]

As part of his staging, Munby chose books which he thought would match Cullwick's character or their shared predicament. He selected Thomas Hardy's lesser-known novel *The Hand of Ethelberta*, 'because it related to people of her own class, and shows them in new positions' (and probably because he was attracted to the 'hand' in the title).[113] Ethelberta is a strong and powerful heroine, the daughter of a servant, who consciously uses marriage as a way of caring for her large family. The narrative is about social mobility, the crossing of classes: Ethelberta is a (secretly) lower-class woman who advances into gentility through marriage, but who then (supposedly) declines in status after her husband's death. Her aim is to advance again through marriage. At one point, she lives as a lady in a large house in London, with her family as her servants (her father butlers for some gentry friends) – a masquerade not dissimilar to that of Cullwick and Munby.[114]

They also read *That Lass o' Lowrie's*, Frances Hodgson Burnett's novel about cross-class love involving a pitwoman who rescues the gentleman she secretly loves from a mining accident. Cullwick read the dialect with ease; Munby thought that she was not unlike Joan Lowrie, the main female character of the novel. Presumably, they appreciated Burnett's exploration of gender contrasts and boundaries: the book includes effeminate men and masculine women, a man with a 'finely cut face ... singularly feminine and innocent', and women who wore 'dress more than half masculine', with strong arms, 'so superb, so statuesque, and yet so womanly'. But Munby and Cullwick would not have approved of the heroine's unease at her ambiguous gender position – 'I'm tired of bein' neyther th' one thing nor th' other. Seems loike I've allus been doin' men's ways, an' I am na content.' We know that they did not like the ending, where Joan refuses to marry her gentleman sweetheart until she has improved herself: 'Give me the time to make myself worthy.'[115] Munby and Cullwick agreed that the author was ignorant about what 'a wench like Joan Lowrie would say and do among gentlefolk'.[116]

Anne Thackeray's *The Village on the Cliff*, published first in serial form in *Cornhill Magazine* in 1866–7, and one of Munby and Cullwick's favourite books, contained startling parallels to their life situation. The name of the main female character in the story is Reine: one of Munby's names for Cullwick was Reine.[117] Reine was a Normandy peasant: Munby bought Cullwick a Normandy peasant costume. Thackeray made Reine of noble descent (as Munby believed Cullwick was). Like Cullwick's, Reine's 'was a striking and heroic type of physiognomy': she was both 'gentle and strong' – 'a rare combination' for women.[118] She looked like 'a princess keeping the cows'.[119] Munby could well have identified with the male protagonist, Richard Butler, who was 'sensitive, artistic, appreciative', a man whose 'tastes were with the aristocracy' while his sympathies were with 'the people'.[120] Then, there was Richard Butler's other love interest, the feminine (and English) Catherine George. She was frail, pretty, childlike – a foil to Reine's strength – 'a blushing, eager little thing' with 'soft little hands'.[121] Although she blushed (on almost every page), she was a governess, not '*de notre classe*', as Richard's relatives expressed it before they sent her away to France to avoid 'the danger of mixin' the different grades of society'.[122] Richard, like Munby, had an attraction for women below him in the social ladder. There are other parallels. Richard, like Munby, drew pictures of the object of his desire. Like Cullwick, Reine always 'made a point of working harder' when her lover was present.[123] Reine did not really look like a peasant; she looked like a lady in peasant costume: the languid, pale figure in the *Cornhill* illustration is not that of a working woman (illus. 37). Cullwick, of course, looked more like the genuine article, but for Munby she was a noble woman in rather deeper disguise. Like Cullwick, Reine disliked dressing in gentry clothes and longed to get back to her 'peasant' dress. She hated the pretension of the upper classes, their reluctance to declare their feelings, and was not afraid to speak her mind to her lover:

Ah, I am no angel from heaven; I have told you that often enough. We in our class are not like you others. We don't pretend to take things as they come, and to care, as you do, for nothing, nor do we women trick our husbands, and speak prettily to them as if they were children to be coaxed and humoured. I have good blood in my veins, but I am a woman of the people for all that, and I love frankness above all things, and there are things belonging to this dress, belonging to rich people I hate, and I always shall hate; never will I condescend to deceive you, to pretend to be what I am not … and if there is anything in my mind, it comes out in time – hatred, or jealousy, or whatever it may be.[124]

This could almost have been Cullwick speaking. Thackeray explored the social gulf between Reine and Richard, '… the gulf she must cross if she did not wish to shock him and repulse him unconsciously at almost every step'. As with Munby and Cullwick, the cross-class jour-

ney was a one-way trip: up for the woman, not down for the man. As
with Munby, Richard was attracted by what he was attempting to
transform: 'He liked her best when he thought of her as herself, at
home in her farm, with her servants and animals round her.'[125] And as
with Cullwick and Munby, Reine was reluctant to marry across class:
'I am ready to die for you, Richard, but I will never marry you – never,
never.'[126]

Munby and Cullwick scripted their lives from fiction, and their
experiences, in turn, helped to shape Munby's art. It was as if Cullwick was being written as she read about the fictional women chosen
by Munby.

VI

One day in 1890, Cullwick finished cleaning Munby's boots, washed
her hands and read aloud 'Queen Kara', a poem he had just
completed.[127] The poem, a curious, racist piece, full of Munby's

phantoms, is about a black slave, Cupassis (evoking the Latin words for desire), used as a footstool by her cruel mistress, Queen Kara, until rescued by a kindly European male to end her days as 'the first black nun'. The oppression of one woman at the hands of another allowed Munby a different charge to the familiar male–female motif. And the story itself, with its Portuguese colonial setting, is far removed from the poet's world. However, the imagery and imaginary will seem very familiar to readers of this chapter, whether it is the grateful slave resting her face on her liberator's foot, or the claim that 'even a slave, obeying, finds reward.'[128] Cupassis's femininity is masked by the scars on her face and the marring blackness of her skin (womanly blushes and red lips are an impossibility).[129] She is degraded, used literally as a footstool, either face down on the floor or on all fours. She is kept naked, apart from

> … her girdle with its thongs,
> And that brass-studded collar of a slave
> Which, more than naked limbs or branded face,
> Reveals a lot as hopeless as the grave.[130]

Cupassis is the lowest of the low. Other slaves are permitted to use her as a 'mat'. She is 'a thing so low, it scarcely dares / To call itself a woman'.[131] (Munby described Cullwick as having '*no inferiors*'.[132]) Yet despite Cupassis's humiliation, there is that essential core of femininity with which Munby was obsessed: 'A slave may sink and yet be womanly.' And, of course, her white saviour helped her to realize this:

> And yet she was a woman now, complete
> With hopes and aspirations, all self-sown,
> And with such finer instincts as were meet
> For the white bosom of a Western Maid.
> Boon Nature gave her all she ought to have;
> Evolving, with the kindly stranger's aid,
> From that crush'd heart and spirit of the slave
> The fragrance of the woman …[133]

She was 'A maid so black, yet, were she only fair, / As beauteous as the best'.[134] So Munby's own Cupassis (who could remove *her* 'disfiguring' blackness) read aloud the erotic fantasies of her master. Did she know what was going on in the mind of the arch stager!

Leopold von Sacher-Masoch's famous novel *Venus in Furs* (1870) tells the story of another Pygmalion, Severin von Kuziemski. His Venus, the beautiful fur-clad Wanda, came to life for his benefit 'like Pygmalion's statue'. She had Grecian features, soft eyes, delicate white skin and 'small transparent hands'. Wanda was the woman of his dreams:

I always carried the image of the ideal woman in my mind; sometimes she appeared on a bed of roses surrounded by Cupids, in a decor of skulls and leather-bound books; sometimes she loomed in Olympian garb, with the severe white face of the plaster Venus.

However, the small, transparent hands of Severin's ideal carried a whip; she taunted him and beat him savagely. And this gentleman contracted himself to be her servant and slave. Their sadomasochistic relationship almost ended in his death as he pursued his desire to be 'the slave of a beautiful woman': 'I want to be able to worship a woman, and I can only do so if she is cruel to me.' The declared philosophy of the tale was that in relationships one had to be either the hammer or the anvil, the dominator or the dominated: 'Man has only one choice: to be a slave or to be a tyrant.' The whole charge of the narrative depended upon the reversal of sexual roles: woman dominating man.[135]

The repertoire of masochism in Sacher-Masoch's novel echoes the imagery of the Munby–Cullwick relationship, and of Munby's sexuality in general: the pleasurable powerlessness of watching a lover with another, and the lover's pleasurable knowledge of that watching; the erotic role of coldness; hands (the hands that hold the whip or clean the floors); foot fetishism (shoes and boots, kissing, the human footstool); woman as divine or demonic, incapable of moderation; the metaphors of 'dog' and 'dog-like'; the objectification of race (Severin is bound by 'Negresses'); and the role of masquerade. Whereas Cullwick and Munby travelled together disguised as equals and assumed the exaggerated master–servant relationship in private, the couple in Sacher-Masoch's tale masqueraded publicly as mistress and servant. Whereas Severin was yoked and harnessed to the plough by his dominatrix, Munby was more interested in yoked milkwomen and ploughing farm girls.

One response might be that Munby had decided to be the hammer; he was the master in masquerade as in real life, and Cullwick was the servant. Their sadomasochism took the form of an exaggeration of their real roles rather than their denial. And yet their relationship was more complex. Munby had anvil-like desires too – as we saw in the descriptions of his delighted feelings of powerlessness in the face of Cullwick's handling by the photographers and her interactions with his tenants. He savoured the switch from mastery to impotence.

Moreover, in Munby's mind, Cullwick was engaged in a double

masquerade. She was not a mere servant degrading herself in over-stated servitude, but a lady in much deeper disguise. This element, missed by so many commentators, provides a different dimension to their association. As Munby wrote in 1898,

Susan and *Ann Morgan's Love*, my two chief poems about her, were said to describe an impossible heroine. Yet she exists; and he who knows what love is, knows that Hannah's whole life has been filled and inspired by it; that this lowly drudge, who is also a lady in disguise, possesses a power of loving, a deep unselfish unswerving lifelong devotion to one object, that has rarely been equalled, & never excelled, in fact or in fiction. He who is that object, may well feel a kind of rapture, in his own long and difficult love for her, and in recording somewhat of her character and work.[136]

The slave was a lady after all.

The poem *Susan* likewise summarized the rationale behind the relationship:

> ... Such a mute maid,
> Whose low condition nothing can degrade
> Save vice, will use each large and sinewy limb
> Of her coarse frame, in drudgery for him
> Who owns her heart, and whose adored commands
> Direct the efforts of her horny hands.
> She makes herself his slave; not that he wills
> She should do thus; but that her passion fills
> The only channel it can hope to find.
> She cannot help him with the equal mind
> Of educated woman; but by this,
> Her own rude work, she can be wholly his:
> Her own rude labour will suffice to show
> The strenuous love that makes her labour so;
> And by its very baseness may express
> Her deep devotion, and her happiness
> In having such a sweetheart for her own.[137]

It is not entirely unpredictable that Munby attributed this slavery to the desires of the slave. The dominator was passive in the face of the power of the dominated. Cullwick was a slave to her love, and expressed this desire in the only way she knew: through work and exaggerated servitude. Munby referred to theirs as 'a marriage of two enthusiasts'. She was an enthusiast for her own class and calling, an enthusiasm which he of course shared. He described himself as an idealist; she was 'the only woman who could fulfil his ideal and who did fulfil it'.[138] The sentence that he enjoyed repeating, reputedly Cullwick's own description, was that their unity existed in their contrast: 'It's the difference, as makes us one': 'From the very first,

84

she delighted in the contrast between her sweetheart's station and her own; between his knowledge and her ignorance; between her large hardworking hands and his hands.' The spheres of contrast were station, mind and body. In this description, written by Munby in 1900, it is significant that once again the agency is attributed to Cullwick. She makes the contrast work through her imagination, unselfishness and love of hard physical work. It is her attributes which 'stimulate this delight'. Thus Munby controlled in a powerfully passive manner: he set the agendas, but constantly attributed agency to the controlee.[139]

Munby claimed that Cullwick had first got the idea of servitude from a dramatization of Byron's poem *King Sardanapalus*, the first play that she had ever seen. The young domestic servant identified with Myrrah, the slave girl who fell in love with her master and was willing to do anything for him: 'I thought, if ever I loved a man, I should like it to be like *that*'; 'I thought, *that's* what I should like! To be sweet heart to one above me, as I could be a slave to, an' him to love me always.'[140]

It is difficult to determine issues of agency in their situation. In 1870, Cullwick wrote that she had forgotten herself for him (these are the terms she used), 'wrapping my soul & body together & giving all to you'.[141] She told him that she liked it when he let her lick his boots (the last three words were erased by Munby, but the excised words almost certainly refer to this practice), and 'especially when you tell me to do it'.[142] It is important to be aware that although much of the detail of this side of their relationship comes from Munby, his knowledge of Cullwick's various humiliations comes from her descriptions. She told him because she knew that it would give him pleasure, but she derived satisfaction from this; it was a complicated situation. Munby was convinced of her enthusiasm for the project. In a letter to Munby, Cullwick described how she had crawled around on the floor on all fours while being kicked by her employers:

'I *liked* it!' she wrote afterwards to her sweetheart; 'I liked to feel that degraded afore 'em all, cause it made me think o' the contrast 'twixt you and me, my Massa!' Expressions of this import – and there are many in her letters – may suffice to show that her submissiveness was not the mere apathy of an abject. It was partly due to her keen sense of her own lowliness and social inferiority to these women, but chiefly, it was the self-sacrifice of a noble nature, rejoicing to suffer for love.[143]

She told her husband that when she was a servant, she had 'licked the gentlefolks' plates' after they had finished with them, and the footmen had mocked her for it – 'Why, you're like a dog!'[144]

Although we know that Cullwick hated some of the tasks that her lover demanded of her – passing as a lady, and recording her daily routine each night before she went to sleep – she was certainly imaginative in initiating new scenarios in their experiment. Early in their relationship, she went to a Margate photographer and asked him to take a photograph of her 'in her dirt'. She blackened her face and arms and had a photograph taken of her polishing a boot. At the photographer's bidding, she also posed as Mary Magdalene (illus. 38): 'He took me in a kneeling position as if praying, with my hair down my back & looking up. The side face was good for it, but the *hands* was too big & coarse he said, so it wouldn't do as a picture.'[145] The description of the interaction between Cullwick and the 'very good-looking' young photographer was provided by her (Munby was never actually present), as was the image of the photograph of her 'in her dirt' exhibited in the photographer's window, alongside those of ladies and gentlemen.[146] The same is true of the myriad of contrasts between Cullwick's large, rough black hands and the tiny white hands of her various employers; of her descriptions of pouring black lead onto her bare hands to blacken the iron grates with her own flesh; and her account of lying face down on the ground with her arms down the outside drain in an attempt to unblock it with her fingers – while her horrified mistress looked on.[147] When they were living together, Cullwick told Munby that on the previous day some visiting working men had been talking 'free' to her, but, as if that was not enough, this had occurred while she was cleaning the toilet: '*I cleaned the closet, before them all!*'[148] Cullwick knew which buttons to press.

Indeed, in his bleaker moments, Munby admitted that his experiment had got out of hand, that Cullwick had taken things further than he had intended. In 1873, when they were living together, Munby referred to the repercussions of his 'strange trials'.[149] In his journal for 1891, he implied that if he had married her sooner, presumably raising her to gentility, the 'tragedy' of their situation could have been avoided. He referred also to her 'moral degradation', by which he meant not sexual promiscuity – for she was 'always' pure – but her 'servile work'.[150] In 1895, he wrote that it had been an 'error that has blighted both their lives; though it has not touched their love': '... he erred greatly, in trying his own purity and hers too much and too long; and in allowing her to call herself his "slave" and his drudge, and to be so, as far as she could.'[151] A far earlier diary for 1860 records Munby's shock when he went to visit Cullwick at work when her mistress was out. She revelled in her dirt because she thought that it pleased him, but he claimed that he was merely saddened by the dete-

38 Hannah Cullwick as
Mary Magdalene:
photograph taken at
Margate, 1864. 'The
side face was good for it,
but the *hands* was to[o]
big & coarse.'

rioration in her appearance during the five years that he had known
her: 'And now, it is high time that all this discipline should cease; but I
have no means of ending it!' This particular entry is important
because it implies that it was Munby who had initially encouraged the
'discipline' and was unable to stop the process once it had begun. As
in the later journal, he regretted not having been in a position to
advance her to the 'drawing room' when he first met her.[152]

Cullwick's diaries suggest the same. On one birthday, she celebrated by crawling into a coal-hole, blacking her face and arms, and
then going to be photographed. The process was recorded for Munby
because she thought that he would like it. She reflected on the previous ten years of their relationship; Munby had taught her the value of
'a contented humble mind' and to be satisfied with her station in life.
She said that she was proud to be his 'slave'. Her phrases about learn-
ing through Munby's teaching, and it having taken ten years for her to
understand, imply his control.[153] We know too from a journal entry
that the initial impetus for climbing up the chimney had been
Munby's: '… you did it just because I ordered you, and out of simple

obedience.'[154] Nevertheless, it is important to realize that the choice that Cullwick remained a servant rather than assuming the identity of a lady was her own: 'Aye Massa … it *would* ha' bin nonsense, you to try an' make a lady o' *me*!'[155] In short, although the sources all conspire against it, we should not underestimate Cullwick's agency in the relationship. We may recall that it was Cullwick herself who said that it was 'painfully delightful to suffer so much for love'.[156] As Munby wrote in one of his poems,

> She was his;
> In mind and heart, his creature and her own;
> But *they* were train'd elsewhere. And presently,
> He learnt, with wonder and a fond surprise,
> How much she knew that he had never taught.[157]

VII

We have encountered several Pygmalions in the course of this chapter: Burne-Jones's, Munby's, Sacher-Masoch's, Shaw's. The painter Jean-Léon Gérôme's *Pygmalion and Galatea* (*c.* 1881) has the sculptor and his creation in a rather erotic embrace, while the Galatea in Honoré Daumier's earlier caricatured *Pygmalion* (1842) asks her creator for a pinch of snuff.[158] The trope was clearly something of a nineteenth and early twentieth-century European cultural commonplace. What Gail Marshall has termed the 'Galatea-aesthetic' informed Victorian art, literature and theatre: woman objectified, quite literally placed on a pedestal as a silent, 'statuesque ideal', and then transformed from marble to flesh by the same desirous male gaze.[159] Indeed, the Pre-Raphaelites, as Deborah Cherry and Griselda Pollock have put it, sought out a procession of working-class women 'as models, lovers and wives, desiring them for their difference, persistently re-forming them and always experiencing anguished conflict over the role and place of these women in the society into which these artists had dragged them'. Women such as Morris's (and Rossetti's) Jane Burden, and Rossetti's Elizabeth Siddal, his *Beata Beatrix*, were fashioned according to the fantasies of the men who knew them, and by the imaginings of generations of (male) art historians and critics.[160] In one ironic moment in 1862, Rossetti espied Munby's hand-tinted photograph of Cullwick, which he immediately took for the portrait of a lady – 'little suspecting who or what she was' (see illus. 19): '"It is a beautiful face" he said "a remarkable face indeed"; & he was anxious to get a copy. "I should like to know that lady" he added. Yes: *that lady*, who is wasting her beauty in drudgery, and who looks no higher than to clean one's boots!'[161]

But there is one more Galatea. Vernon Lee's novel *Miss Brown* (1884) is a story about a wealthy Pre-Raphaelite poet and painter, Walter Hamlin, who decides to raise a servant employed by his friend. The intention is to educate and then marry the young woman. He would save the beautiful Anne Brown from the life she is destined to lead as a servant and turn her into a thing of beauty: 'Either Anne Brown must turn into a sordid nursery-governess, or into the avowedly most beautiful woman in England – that is to say, in the particular pre-Raphaelite society which constituted England to him.' She would be his Galatea: 'Walter Hamlin's life should be crowned by gradually endowing with vitality, and then wooing, awakening the love of this beautiful Galatea whose soul he had moulded, even as Pygmalion had moulded the limbs of the image which he had made to live and to love.'[162] Hamlin settles a substantial portion on her so that she can achieve a certain degree of independence after her schooling in order to be in a position to decide whether or not she wishes to marry him. But she feels trapped, obligated, in bondage, a slave.

The gender reversals in the novel are uncannily familiar. Hamlin has 'girlish beauty': his femininity, and the femininity of his circle, contrasts with Brown's masculinity. Like so many of Munby's women, Anne Brown is a hybrid: a 'beautiful and dramatic creature' with a 'superb physical appearance'. When Hamlin first sees her, she is ironing, and his eyes are drawn to her arms, 'her bare brown arms going up and down along the board; her massive and yet girlish body bending with the movement'. She is described as 'no woman at all, but a mere sexless creature'; 'Some few women seem to be born to have been men, or at least not to have been women.' Her nose is 'massive', a sign of her masculinity and power.[163]

There are interesting parallels with Munby and Cullwick. Hamlin writes poems 'upon the strange fate which had, to put it in plain prose, given the beauty of an Amazon to a nursemaid'. He selects her reading. The novel is full of watching: 'He looked at her with the curiosity of an artist examining a model.' He watches her at the opera. He sketches her. He observes her interactions with others. Hamlin constructs Anne Brown as an ideal, projecting his desires onto her and treating her like an artist's model: 'There was not much perception of the reality of Anne Brown's personality, nor indeed of her having any personality at all, being a thing with feelings, thoughts, hopes, interests of her own.' He even designs her dresses in keeping with Pre-Raphaelite aesthetics.[164]

At one point in the novel, Anne tells herself that Hamlin had wanted 'to make her into the highest thing which a man can make a woman – a sort of Beatrice, a creature to love whom will be spiritual redemption'.[165] The interest in this Galatea is that, as Hilary Fraser has recently observed, she provides the occasion for a critique of male voyeurism: 'It reveals Lee's acute awareness of woman as spectacle in the contemporary visual economy.'[166] Even if Anne Brown eventually marries Walter Hamlin, she repeatedly troubles the fantasy: 'Did he care for her only as a sort of living picture?'[167] Of course, the creator of this rather unsettling Galatea was a woman. Vernon Lee was a pseudonym; her real name was Violet Paget.[168]

4 Disordering Bodies: Gender Hybridity

I

In 1871, when Arthur Munby was leaving a money-changer's in the Haymarket, a figure crossed his path, 'so different, so suggestive, so attractive to me that it brightened all things' (illus. 39, 40): 'It was only a milkwoman: but such a perfect milkwoman.' She was tall, sunburnt, 'robust', 'erect and graceful with a rustic grace'. She wore a modest bonnet, neat shawl, short lilac frock and 'snowy white' stockings with 'massive manly ankleboots'. Her broad hands were muscular yet 'feminine still'.

As for her face, it was a sweet and placid face of regular feature and rich apricot complexion, touched with work and time a little, and yet still young and blooming; with smooth dark hair laid close to the round forehead: the face of a pure and honest working woman, apparently; serene and self reliant.

She was a goddess among the 'evil men and monstrous apish girls of that market quarter'.[1]

Munby saw a 'milkwench' in Jermyn Street in 1863, talking to a labouring man. He sketched the figures (illus. 41), evoking the contrasts that fastened on the scene: the massive size of the woman beside the puny man. He fetishized the woman's strength and independence, and focused on the objects of his fetishism: large limbs, boots and brown arms. The woman's exposed legs – which we would scarcely notice – were erotic objects.[2] He captured other contrasts in a picture sketched in 1869 of himself standing next to his favourite milkwoman, 'Rosyface'. The rather crude sketch is of a harnessed, stocky, dark, huge-handed, big-booted working woman, shaking hands with an unencumbered, slender, pale, small-handed, tiny-shoed gentleman (illus. 42). The two figures are of roughly equal height, though the man's top hat makes him look taller.[3]

Milkwomen were 'full of contradictions'.[4] Yet Munby saw gender ambiguities not just between the massive women and small men, but in the very bodies of the women themselves – in their own bodily

39, 40 Milkwomen: Note the contrast between the sketch and photograph – an indication of the way in which Munby viewed the bodies of these women, and a measure of his fetishism.

41, 42 Contrasts: masculine
women and feminine men
sketched by Munby in the
1860s.

contradictions of refined expectations of masculinity and femininity. When we look at Munby's sketch of the Jermyn Street milkwoman, most of us will see a ridiculously large female form. But Munby saw a 'noble figure':

... her make was brawny and massive, but lithe and shapely withal; and it was set off to the utmost by her milkwoman's dress. For she wore no shawl, but only a checked woollen kerchief that served to show the breadth of her broad shoulders, and the width of her ample waist; and her muscular brown arms were bare; and her pink apron and stuff skirt were as usual so short, that the calf of her stout whitestocking'd leg was well seen, above her well-blacked, bignailed, and enormous boots ... She stood erect and stalwart & independent, in the attitude of a dragoon, but with a flowing ease at every turn of her large limbs, that was all feminine: exquisitely clean and wholesome in person and dress; ineffably rustic and unpretending in manner: a superb colossal woman ...[5]

Above all, the milkwoman represented the consummate combination of masculinity and femininity; she was both womanly and unwomanly. Thus the hybridity of 'Young Mary', whose photograph is in Munby's collection.[6] She was 'robust but most feminine', her yoke, heavy cans and large ankle-boots contrasting with her 'soft', 'tender' and 'comely' face. Like her fellows, she was 'full of health and rustic vigour': 'A charming portrait of a working lass, as womanly as she is laborious'.[7] He provided a similar description of another milkwoman in 1872 as 'charmingly rural and picturesque', with a 'soft peachbloom' complexion 'heightened by contrast' with her 'rude laborious arms'.[8]

The title of this chapter — 'Disordering Bodies' – refers to Judith Butler's now classic theoretical destabilizing of sex and gender. Much recent work on identity has thrown binary certainties into doubt, questioning not only any direct and necessary correspondence between sex and gender, but arguing that sex itself is a gendered category. Gender, in this new conceptual framework, is best considered as performance, 'a corporeal style'.[9] The implications of this destabilizing are immense. 'If sex does not limit gender', Butler has written,

then perhaps there are genders, ways of culturally interpreting the sexed body, that are in no way restricted by the apparent duality of sex. Consider the further consequence that if gender is something that one becomes – but can never be – then gender is itself a kind of becoming or activity ... an incessant and repeated action ... that can potentially proliferate beyond the binary limits imposed by the apparent binary of sex.[10]

There are several ways of demonstrating the non-fixity of gender, the possibility, as Butler has expressed it, referring to the fiction of Monique Wittig, of becoming a being 'whom neither *man* nor *woman* truly describes':

> This is not the figure of the androgyne nor some hypothetical 'third gender', nor is it a *transcendence* of the binary. Indeed, it is an internal subversion in which the binary is both presupposed and proliferated to the point where it no longer makes sense.[11]

Most discussions of the possibilities of what has become known as 'gender fucking' (or 'genderfuck') are firmly post-modern, 'Fin de siècle, fin de sexe': either figures of cyber fiction, literary invention, and film and video, or pop and performance artists, surgically transformed 'trans-intersexuals', and a range of practitioners of queer sex (leatherdyke boys and leatherdyke daddies, for example).[12] My intention is to show that it is possible to turn to the nineteenth century for examples of 'neither man nor women' figures. These disordering bodies are Munby's representations: the milkwomen, female acrobats and coalmine workers of his 'sociological' studies. They provide a novel glimpse of gender hybridity in Victorian England.

II

A number of critics have noted Munby's fascination with gender transgression. In the words of Anne McClintock, 'What entranced him was the spectacle of boundaries crossed – that titillating moment when woman was confused with man and man with woman. The voyeuristic spectacle of cross-dressing held him entirely in its thrall.'[13] At one extreme, there was indeed the woman who passed as a man. Munby kept a file on these cross-dressers.[14] In 1866, he tracked down Richard Bruce, a woman who had entered the workhouse as a male tramp. The woman told him that she had first started dressing as a man to earn better wages and had worked in various male guises – including at the docks and in an ironstone mine. She had lived in London as a man, staying in lodging houses, and informed the curious Munby that she planned to get work as a (male) piano player in the music halls. Munby thought that she looked like 'a strong lad in petticoats'.[15] He saw Thomas Walker charged with embezzlement in Southwark Police Court. Walker, who had worked variously as a ship's steward, porter and barman, was a woman who had cut her hair short to pass as a man. Munby described her as 'bluff and brawny', with a bull-neck and square shoulders. When she appeared in court, she wore a petticoat as a symbol of her real sex, but to all appearances she was a man from the waist up; as s/he stood in the dock in her blue sailor's shirt with the sleeves rolled up, 'it was almost impossible to believe that she was not a man.' No-one had detected her passing until she was confronted with the prison bath.[16]

A woman passing as a man was only one form of crossing.[17] Other women were interesting not because of any deliberate masquerade on their part, but because their labour masculinized their bodies (illus. 43, 44). Their passing was unconscious. Munby described

the gangs of dustwomen stalking through the park, with their great bundles on their heads, gigantic in the mist; scarce to be distinguished from men with their big rough coats, rough voices, and loud trampling feet; strong manly women with smeared faces & hard hands; painful, very, to the civilized beholder![18]

These large, dirty women moved en masse, powerfully, 'bearing down upon one ... like Birnam Wood on its way to Dunsinane'.[19] Munby was taken with the irony that these strong dustwomen were suppos-edly of the 'gentler sex'. He thought them 'charmingly barbarous'; they 'so exquisitely contrasted with the ways of one's own class'.[20] Dustwomen were 'masculine', 'manlike'.[21] They wore men's coats – some were even clad in the cast-off dress coats of the upper classes.[22] Munby was intrigued by the ways in which working women trans-gressed middle- and upper-class notions of femininity, not only in their appearance, but in their physical power:

> ... these creatures masculine:
> Rough servant girls, whom nothing can refine;
> The black and rugged wenches of the mine;
> The sunburnt damsels of the field or farm;
> All, who by force of bulk and strength of arm
> Can keep a bad man's insolence at bay,
> And make him feel that they, and such as they,
> Can hold their own unaided.[23]

He sought out counterpoints to the feminine ideal.

What I want to argue here, though, is that such straightforward 'crossing of sex lines'[24] is less interesting than the intermediate possi-bilities, and that the scope for these other combinations was rich and varied. For Munby was even more intrigued by what is best described as gender hybridity. We can see this quite clearly in his representation of the Shropshire pit women who were seasonally employed in the market gardens of Middlesex. His description of them begins with first impressions, feinting a simple gender inversion, the binary image of the erasure of femininity: 'strong brown Shropshire women', wearing lettered sacking, moving 'like men, stalwart and large &

43, 44 Photograph of a Lambeth
dustgirl, 1862, and Munby's sketch
of a Paddington dustwoman.
Again, note the exaggerated
drawing.

sunburnt'. But it is the imagery of intermixture – indeed of gender blending – which dominates. One woman, whom Munby singled out and conversed with in dialect, was clad in a coarse smock, shawl, potato-sack petticoat, stockings (visible to the knee) and huge clay-covered boots. She was tall and strong, with broad shoulders and stout legs, and walked 'with great strides, swinging her arms like a ploughman'. Yet there were also traces of femininity. As Munby glossed, the woman was 'not unfeminine'. She sang with a 'fresh' and 'girlish' voice, had blue eyes (a sure sign of femininity), was 'comely' and possessed hands which, 'though broad and thick were delicate looking for one who works with hoe and spade'. Indeed, the dirt on her face was an aid to eroticization and objectification: '... there was a significant daub of clay on either side of her shapely retrousse nose.'[25]

Hester Burdon, a Yorkshire farm servant, had done all the tasks of male agricultural labour, including ploughing:

> ... here is a young woman who has been brought up from a child in the stable and field and farmyard; among cart horses and dungheaps and pigstyes: who has lived as a ploughman and day labourer, changing almost her very sex ... and after ten years of this training, what is she like? Why, this ploughwench is an exceedingly pretty girl, with a feminine face and bright intelligent character, and with a figure and air as neat and womanly as you will see in a day's walk; only her hands being – what they are and ought to be. And this sordid spreader of dung, this female groom and horsetaming Amazon, is a wife who has found her married life the happiest part of her existence.[26]

A pretty young potato picker – whose fellow workers Munby had mistaken for a herd of cattle – was described as a virgin beauty amidst 'deep earth and rough clods':

> A female day labourer – a rough wench gathering taters with her fellows in the open field ... And yet she, being or looking thus, had such an artless sweetness in her girlish face, such an air of purity & maidenhood about her ... that no amount of culture could have made her a nobler woman ... her presence, the presence of a country lass in a smock frock and hobnailed boots, gave a sort of drawing room perfume to the rude potato field.

She reflected Munby's ideal in women: 'the beauty of honest healthful labour, and that of elegant female grace, redoubling each other by their union'. In her was 'that mixture of manly frankness and womanly delicacy' that Munby so admired in working women.[27]

We can see similar combinations at work in Munby's descriptions of the Filey and Flamborough 'flither lasses' who, sometimes in appalling wintry conditions, climbed sheer cliffs with ropes to bring up stones, bait and driftwood. They had a masculine appearance, particularly from a distance. They did hard physical work, rolling their skirts up like breeches to facilitate climbing – Munby revelled in such descriptions of muscularity and strength. But it was brawn combined with femininity (illus. 45). One of these young women, who had just ascended a cliff, was described as 'a bloomin bonny lass of seventeen, with a childlike face just blushing into womanhood'[28]: 'It is something to know and see ... that there are girls in England who can swarm up ... 300 & 400 feet of ship's rope & sea crag.'[29]

Finally, there were the domestic servants whose hands declared the nature of their work. Munby's diary for 1861 contains his recollections of a visit to Yatton when he met the servant Elizabeth Shepstone. He noticed her hands from across the room:

I asked her to show me her hand. Staring at me in blank astonishment, she obeyed, and held out her right hand for me to look at. And certainly, I never saw such a hand as hers, either in man or woman. They were large and thick & broad, with big rude fingers and great bony thumbs – but that was not very remarkable: they were coarse and red and rough-ribbed on the outside, and covered moreover with clumps of large warts – that was somewhat remarkable, but not unique. It was in her *palms* that she was unrivalled: and such

45 'Flither lasses' photographed in 1871. Note the trousers and exposed legs.

palms! The whole interior of each hand, from the wrist to the finger-tips, was *hoofed* with a thick sheet of horn.

The relevance of these hands is that they accompanied many of the signs of conventional femininity. 'And', Munby continued in his account of Shepstone, 'the piquant thing was, that with all this she was young and pretty: a rural belle, with bright eyes & rosy cheeks and dimpled golden hair: robust and strong indeed, but far from being coarse or clumsy in make or manner.' 'I examined this monstrous phenomenon with the greater amazement, because of the blooming girlish face of its owner ... The combination of such a face and such a hand was one that I had often thought of as desirable; but I never expected to see it more than realized.'[30] His poem 'Elizabeth Shepstone', written much later, in 1889, similarly recounts the enormity of her hands, but again to highlight her essential femininity. Elizabeth had 'monstrous' hands, but soft brown hair, rosy cheeks, bright eyes and a 'girlish countenance'. She blushed when Munby asked her about a sweetheart:

> ... thus looking at her fair young face –
> Her frank blue eyes, her sunny cheeks, her lips
> All ripe for love, her soft brown feminine hair
> Parted amidst, as woman's hair should part,
> Above a smooth white brow; and in all these
> Seeing the grace of youth and womanhood ...
> Those very hands from which I shrank with scorn,
> Those hands of hers, by necessary toil
> Made horny and repulsive, came to be
> An adjunct of her beauty; lending it
> The force of contrast ...[31]

The hands of servants, then, were sufficient to subvert the other signs of these women's essential femininity, providing the combination of 'such a face and such a hand', the contrast which formed Munby's obsession. The hands of servants declared their bodily hybridity. These pretty labourers in hobnailed boots, ploughmen with *retroussé* noses and servants with soft brown hair and horny hands were, quite literally, gender hybrids.

III

Much post-modern representation of gender fucking focuses on the naked form: the body with a penis and large breasts; the muscular (masculine) body without breasts and penis; the woman with a strap-on dildo. Bodies are rearranged and, literally, bared in defiance of gendered expectations. Such blatant nudity was absent from Munby's men/women. However, exposed hands, legs, feet and faces acted as synecdoches in an equally powerful statement about hidden bodies. Gender hybridity was achieved through combinations and tricked anticipations of clothing and bodies in ways that, while not as blatant as genderfuck, were certainly challenging in the context of their time.

Let us start with a form of nakedness. Munby was extremely interested in female acrobats, and frequently sketched them (illus. 46). His drawings were meant to capture the shock of their virtual nakedness and bodily contortions, subverting preconceived notions of feminine comportment and demeanour. '[A] year ago', he wrote in 1868, 'it would have seemed incredible that my sketch above is a faithful picture of an English girl, as she appears nightly before an applauding London audience.'[32] A primary attraction was that these women, who could be very pretty and ladylike in facial expression, performed – in a state of virtual undress – very unladylike feats of strength and bodily contortion, suspending themselves upside down (illus. 47), swinging from ropes, dropping from the sky, even being shot out of a cannon. An acrobat at the Oxford Music Hall supported her husband on her head and their child on his head.[33] Another acrobat, who performed at the Westminster Aquarium, hung upside down from a trapeze, with a rubber thong between her teeth, holding the weight of three men.[34] This was a spectacular flaunting of Victorian domestic ideals: 'It is something, to see a wife turn a somersault over her husband's head, & both of them nearly nude.'[35]

46 Female acrobats drawn by Munby in 1868.

It is important to be aware that the nakedness of the female acrobat was not mere undress. The performer Lulu was 'drest – or undrest – as an acrobat' in what Munby described as 'male attire': 'pink flesh-ings and trunkhose and tight sleeveless blue doublet'.[36] Mme Stertzenbach of the Alhambra was dressed 'like a male acrobat', indeed identically to her husband, who performed with her. Her hair was also cut short like a man's. Her legs, 'up to the very hips, were (so to say) naked, being clothed only in tight fleshings that showed every muscle'. The tights of the female acrobats were a form of cross-dress-ing; they undermined the wearer's sex while revealing it. The perfor-mances of these women were exercises in gender ambiguity. Man and woman appeared almost indistinguishable (illus. 48): 'I have never seen a more complete abnegation of sex.'[37]

Munby saw Zazel at the Westminster Aquarium on two successive occasions in 1877. She walked a tightrope, rode the trapeze, leaped 60 feet into a net, and was shot out of a cannon. He was attracted by her combination of comeliness, strength and daring, her 'gracefully exerted power'. Munby seemed particularly intrigued by Zazel's after-performance transformation into 'a respectable tradesman's

48 Mme Senyah, acrobat, and husband, 1868: The Hayneses performed as the Senyahs in the London music halls.

daughter'. True to form, he followed her when she left the Aquarium to take her brother and sister to get something to eat. Zazel was both male and female: an ordinary, modest young woman, whom one would pass in the street without comment, with the body of a muscular performer.[38]

Another favourite was the child gymnast Nathalie Foucart. Munby also saw her at the Alhambra, in male clothing, and with a figure 'that of a boy'. She dazzled him with her acrobatics on the trapeze. Familiar themes emerge: gender ambiguity in form and actions; strength ('muscular power which would have been wonderful in a man'); bodily contortion, recorded by Munby in sketches of these 'most unnatural' positions. He managed to meet her afterwards and even to shake her hand. The performance continued for Munby in the contrast between her on- and off-stage persona, for away from the Alhambra she was a 'quiet little schoolgirl in a brown frock and straw hat, walking between her father and her mother': 'I have described all this climbing and tumbling and muscular effort, because it was done not by a man or even a boy, arduous as it was, but by a female performer, and her a mere child.'[39] Munby saw Foucart perform again in 1864 with her two younger sisters. They were dressed in boys' clothes (shirts and velvet breeches), with their hair parted on one side like males. They performed 'muscular masculine feats'. Munby captured the moment with a tiny thumbnail sketch of Nathalie hanging upside down, posterior facing the viewer, and with her boyish haircut visible through her trousered legs. [40]

As with other spectators of female public performance, it was the contradictions of female display which so appealed. What Tracy Davis has written of actresses is equally applicable to female acrobats: '... the theatre required of them a curious mixture of assertiveness and self-negation, flamboyance and modesty ... and active and reactive qualities.'[41] If, as one contemporary put it, the stage was 'an abrupt emancipation from the fetters ... of the domestic vassalage', how much more of a disruption acrobatics would have been![42] Like actresses, female acrobats 'defeminized' themselves on the public stage. They exhibited their bodies, for the pink tights that acrobats and dancers wore signified nakedness. As Munby observed of a harlequinade performer, fleshings gave the appearance of nudity – to the waist, if the performer was above eye-level.[43] Fractured femininity was revealed in the sexuality of display, and in Munby's descriptions and denials of degradation and immodesty. The harlequinade performer at Covent Garden appeared 'apparently nude' and was suspended in spotlight 'rigid and helpless as the knob on the end of a barber's pole', 'illuminated there for the benefit of a thousand gazers'. Yet she 'looked comely and respectable'.[44] In short, she had all the attributes of femininity while simultaneously shattering them.

IV

It is clear that colliery women were another major preoccupation of Munby's. He collected them; he refers tellingly to one woman as a specimen. Their names – scores of them – are underlined in his diaries, with brief descriptions of their appearance and the manner of their meeting. In one day in 1880, he visited a dozen pits and counted over 90 women, nearly all of whom, he noted in his diary's table, were young.[45] He recorded his quarry's heights. He sketched them (more on this later), sometimes as nightmarish caricatures, sometimes including a self-portrait to emphasize contrasts. He purchased their photographs and paid them to pose for new images: his collection of images of pitwomen is a major archive. He felt free to quiz and pen intimate ethnographies of their lives and living situations. What were the sleeping arrangements in their homes? How often did they wash? Did they bathe all over, and did the coal dust get under their clothes?[46] In one remarkable episode, he persuaded one woman (Ellen Grounds) to let him examine her trousers. His journal records their appearance: an old pair of men's breeches, they were patched in various colours with cotton and linen, and coloured black-brown by coal dust. They were lined and padded at the knees. And, Munby noted in a passage seized on by a modern critic, 'the *inside* of the trousers was clean'.[47] The fetishist got to handle the object of his desire in front of the wearer, with no apparent hint of offence. Such were the arrogances of class. The Lancashire women called Munby 'th' inspector'.[48]

In the Wigan area, Munby could witness female labour en masse:

… as I stood on the brow at Douglas Bank and looked on that crowd of rough and busy workers, and saw stalwart labourers striding along the railway with spade on shoulder, or climbing up the sides of the trucks, and standing on the trucks, shovelling the coal into its place and fixing the big coals with their hands around the edges of the truck, or moving up & down, like sweeps in a chimney, within the darkness of the steep coalshoots, or thrutching corves from the pit mouth, amid clouds of coaldust, or running them down the breezy incline – and as I realized with difficulty the fact that nearly all these muscular black people in coats and trousers were young women …[49]

He enjoyed the tricks that his eyes played: figures that he was convinced must be male turned out to be women (illus. 49): 'I found that this great masculine figure was a young girl, not unfeminine at all, except in dress.'[50] 'Whenever a party approached, one had to guess which were men & which women; and sometimes they proved to be all women.' Sometimes, it was only the pink kerchief which proclaimed the gender of the wearer.[51] One of those he sketched in 1865 was Alice Gosling,

aged 17, a perfect beauty; brunette, with rosetint blushing through; dark grey eyes, pouting lips, & most sweet smile. She had her bonnet off; her black hair, soft bright abundant, was smooth brushed … her face was scarce soiled … her bare arms, round & shapely, had their lustrous brown just roughened with coal dust. The palms of her hand were quite black, of course: but the hands themselves feminine. Her pink shirt was patched till it looked like a patchwork quilt; her trousers very short, showing a full calf cased in warm grey stocking. Sitting thus on the rude bench, arms folded and feet crossed, she made one of the most charming & picturesque figures I ever saw hereabouts. I sketched her on the sly as I talked: *she* didn't know, poor dear, what the book & pencil meant![52]

(The sketch presents her as rather pale compared to some of the other representations.) The pitwomen were hybrid creatures, combining

49 Ellen Lowe, aged 22, collier: '... a girl wholly and intensely black, but bonny & gentle withal: and a white lad with her'.

male and female postures and attributes. Gosling's folded arms and crossed legs were signs of masculinity, but this demeanour accompanied pouting lips and a sweet smile (men did not pout and smile sweetly). In an 1866 description of a group of women resting, Munby fastened on the contrast between their limbs and their heads: iron-clad feet, 'stout masculine legs' and muscular arms that 'a navvy might own', coupled with 'girlish heads' of plaited shining hair, earrings and neck-ribbons (illus. 50, 51).[53]

It is difficult for us to read back into these pictures. When we look at the drawings or photographs of the pitwomen, or the drawing of Munby and Mary Harrison walking along the road (illus. 52), we merely see women in trousers. But for Munby, and for all the middle-class collectors of photographs of collier women, these would have been images of women in men's clothing – which also revealed their limbs.[54] If we were discussing men, we might refer to them being unmanned. Yet there is no strictly equivalent phrase for women: *defeminized* is not quite the right word. Pitwomen were unwomaned. This unwomaning occurred in two major ways: in their work, and in their appearance – more specifically, in their dress and in their blackness.

106

50, 51 Pitwomen: group photograph, 1867, and author's close-up. Observe the earrings, hair and hands.

52 Arthur Munby and Mary Harrison: This sketch would have had added meaning for Munby, for he gave the woman sixpence as they parted, pressing the coin into her hand. His drawing would have reminded him of the fetishized contact: 'The sixpence lay, glittering white, in the dull black palm of her extended right hand. I touched that dull black palm; it was rough and very hard. I looked in its owner's womanly face and said "You have a good hard hand!" "Aye, Sir", the maiden answered meekly, "it is hard."'

The first way in which pit work unwomaned, recounted mainly in memories by the time Munby was carrying out his investigations, was with the work that women had done underground, drawing corves on all fours like animals. This imagery provided an obvious subversion of femininity: 'I was harnessed to the corves, with a belt round my body and the chain between my legs ... And you went on your hands and feet, just as a horse goes on four legs?'[55] One woman, who had been underground for fifteen years, showed Munby how it was done, crouching on the ground on all fours: 'Yes, it was like a horse or a dog; and it was the same with us as them; it was a second nature to us, like, and we thought no more of it than them wenches do of digging for coal.'[56]

The clothing of pitwomen played an obvious role in their bodily disorder. When Munby met Ellen Grounds in her pit clothes to have her photographed, he thought that she looked much bigger than when she wore a dress. He described her size as filling the portrait shed. She had not brought her coat with her so had to wear one of the photographer's husband's jackets.[57] She was given a spade to represent the pit shovel (so much for verisimilitude). Munby stood next to

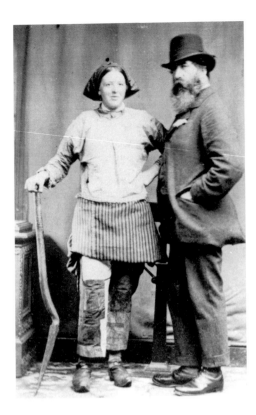

her to show her size (illus. 53). The photographs took an hour; in
between poses, Ellen nursed her child. At the end of the session, she
let down her pit skirt (which had been hitched up around her
trousers) and put on a petticoat and an apron. They took another
picture of her holding a broom; she has all the appearance of a domestic servant. Ellen laughed at the pose without her bonnet and said that
it made her look like she was sweeping the house.[58] As Griselda
Pollock has argued, the contrast between the pictures with the skirt
down and the skirt up contains a cue to reading trousered women: not
as women wearing trousers, but as women with their skirts up, with
the shape of their legs exposed. The rolled-up petticoat that the
collier women wore over their trousers was intended, Munby
explained in 1859, merely as a symbol of their sex.[59] To quote Pollock,
'They walked about in public with their skirts hitched up – and
although their legs are encased in rough men's trousers, these function as a sheaf, like the tights worn by ballet dancers and acrobats ...
which drew attention to the legs while also veiling them' (illus. 54).[60]
But we can take the reading a little further than Pollock. Another
important aspect of the viewing is the gender ambiguity, the cross-

54 Female collier, Rose Bridge
Pits, 1869.

dressing. These women did not merely have their skirts up, but their legs were encased in *male* clothing. There was, if you like, a double charge, perhaps even more powerful than the fictional nakedness of the female acrobats discussed earlier.

It is instructive to compare the imagery in Munby's various texts with the reactions of other outsiders to show just how threatening these manly women could be. An article in *Once A Week* paraded the insecurities. The women in this discourse are unambivalently 'unwomanly' apart from tell-tale signs of 'feminine weakness' in the form of earrings and a bonnet: '"These", said he, "are men, not women".' The author could not even bring himself to name the signifiers of this masculinity: trousers were 'patched fustian unmentionables'. The women were not individuals but wives and daughters. Their work presented a 'degrading spectacle', a 'spectacle utterly repugnant'. In such discourse, trousers represent their female wearers' abandonment of 'the characteristic modesty and purity of their sex'. They signify not only unwomanliness, but moral depravity (illegitimacy and drunkenness) and the abandonment of domestic duties.[61]

However, the most important trope in Munby's representations of pitwomen was the theme of marred beauty. Blackness/dirt disfigured the beauty of these women. His attitude to them was identical to his reaction to (and fascination with) the female minstrels who performed in London streets and music halls (see illus. 7). These performers, with their blackened faces, necks, ears, arms and hands, were, he wrote, 'Deprived thus of all feminine charms'.[62] Blackness 'completely destroyed' their beauty. When a woman disported herself as a minstrel, 'the first thing we think of is her degradation and disfigurement.'[63] What Munby termed 'selfmade negresses' disguised whatever good looks they may have had; he saw such performances as an abandonment of 'the feminine desire to be good-looking'.[64]

Blackness similarly robbed the pitwomen of their features. It defeminized them. But the theft was only skin deep, for beneath it lay a hidden beauty. This is apparent in Munby's description and sketch of Eliza Hayes. She was, he wrote, feminine in her speech and manner, but 'by all outward signs' more of a man than her male companion:

She was, as far as I could judge, a robust and goodlooking lass, though as usual she had lost all her front teeth: but she was about the very blackest pitwench I ever saw. Her very eyeballs seemed sprinkled with coaldust: her nostrils and her ears were full of it: and every inch of her face and neck was thickly overlaid with a dull Satanic blackness, reflecting no light, but masking all her features as if with a veil. En revanche however, when this grinning girl opened her mouth to speak, her gums (she had no front teeth, as I have said) and the inner surface of her lips, glowed by contrast with a moist & lovely pink, clean and bright as the lip of a sea shell. Her hands of course were as black as her face; and her neck kerchief & coat and trousers were almost as sooty as herself. Could any one fall in love with such a girl? Why not, if he waited till she was washed?

This is a remarkable description of penetrating the façade of blackness.[65] It was the soft, pink femininity within that Munby fetishized.

The description becomes even more unsettling and bizarre when combined with his visual portrayal of the young collier. Anne McClintock has read the racial text embodied in the drawing of Eliza Hayes. The gender crossings are plain in the sketch of the pale, effete Munby next to the sturdy black Hayes (illus. 55). Everything about the upper-class man is feminine in comparison to the strong working-class woman. As McClintock wrote, 'His entire appearance has an aura of frailty, an almost invalid-like vulnerability next to the colliery woman's sturdy bulk.' But there is an equally strong racial component: Hayes is not only masculine in appearance; she is also black:

She presents a grotesque caricature of the stigmata of racial degeneration:

her forehead is flattened and foreshortened; the whites of her eyes stare
grotesquely from her black face; her lips are artificially full and pale. Her
neck is sunk into her shoulders; her hands are hugely simian, black and
improbably large.[66]

Griselda Pollock has likewise discussed the racist stereotyping in such
sketches.[67] It is not my purpose to challenge such readings of the
disturbing racial implications of Munby's imagery (illus. 56, 57). We
know that his descriptions of the pitwomen – black women, black
faces, black necks, black arms, black hands, 'big black wenches' –
continually slip into descriptions of race.[68] However, both commentators missed Munby's fetishization of concealed femininity: the
'woman's heart within her man's waistcoat' and the 'woman's beauty
under the soot that covered her'.[69] The situation was more complex
than McClintock and Pollock allowed. Even in the unsexed black
Eliza Hayes Munby detected femininity.[70] It was gender rather than
race that was of prime concern to this investigator.

The pitwomen, then, were archetypal gender hybrids. Munby
thought Ellen Grounds 'comely', his word of bodily approval, and
referred to her aquiline features, blue eyes, and red lips and white

56, 57 Race and gender: more examples of Munby's disturbing images of disfigurement through blackness.

58, 59 Masculine/feminine: photographs of
Ellen Grounds in masculine working and
feminine leisure dress; blush was added to her
cheeks in the bottom photograph to
emphasize her femininity.

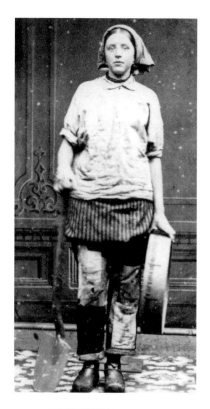

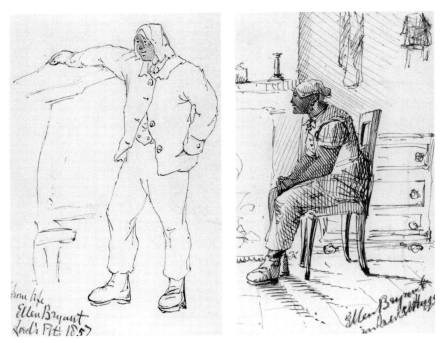

60, 61 Munby's drawings of Ellen Bryant in 1857.

62 Working-class motherhood:
Mary Ann Morgan nursing her
baby, 1866.

teeth contrasting with the coaldust of her cheeks. His descriptions of her constantly slip from masculinity to femininity, and he collected photographs to illustrate this theme (illus. 58, 59). She looks at him as a man might look at a man. She is a 'manlike' girl, like a 'strong brave son', but with pale chestnut hair and a white forehead. She wore trousers, but had long braided hair. He watched her ascend the stairs into her loft in male attire and then come down again, shortly afterwards, in a dress, transformed into a woman.[71] Mary Anne Atkinson looked 'like some sexless creature – a collier-angel'.[72] Olive Swift was a girl with 'a handsome Eastern face, with large lustrous eyes and aquiline profile, such as you see in Egyptian sculptures ... What a face, to be daubed with coal dust, to belong to a lass who wears breeches'.[73] During a break in their labours, Munby heard pitgirls singing ballads about courtship and tragic love. The sight of trousered and begrimed women, with their muscular arms around one another, singing like angels, thrilled the seasoned observer: 'Consider the pathos of those girls' laborious lives and the beauty of their singing.'[74]

Munby was fully cognisant of the mixed gender of these northern working women: witness his drawings of Ellen Bryant, for example (illus. 60, 61). Jane Cave was

tall and robust ... with a handsome and finely moulded face; a straight high-bred nose, a full firm chin, and a beautiful rosebud mouth, the upper lip thin and the under full and pouting: fair hair and blue eyes, and a rich apricot skin, darkened but little by coal dust ... she stood erect, in her fustian trousers and clogs, her hands in the pockets of her thick top coat.

Cave was a perfect hybrid. Her masculinity was reflected in her clothing and her stance: her femininity resided in her mouth and skin. She was a 'manlike woman'.[75] Munby described Mary Ann Morgan, nursing her fatherless baby: '... it was odd to see that little white baby clasped by the brown brawny arm and the black hand, & sucking at the breast of a strong hybrid creature in (one may say) men's clothes.' The sketch (illus. 62) which accompanies the journal entry is of a powerful woman in trousers, cradling a tiny baby about the same size as one of her hands or boots. It is a strange but compelling image of working-class motherhood.[76]

V

There is nothing marginal about the imagery and cultural crossings we have been exploring. We have to resist seeing such worlds as hidden, as the underside of Victorianism. Dustwomen, milkwomen and servants were commonplace. Pitwomen were visible to any visitor to Wigan or Wales (illus. 63, 64), or to readers of Frances Hodgson Burnett's *That Lass o' Lowrie's*, with its 'half masculine' women, strong-armed, womanly beings, 'tired of bein' neyther th' one thing nor th' other'.[77] The woman passing as a man was hardly an unknown phenomenon in the nineteenth century.[78] The sexually ambiguous performers of the music halls were certainly ubiquitous.[79] Anyone could go to a pantomime and see a woman transformed into a cat, 'throwing off her womanhood' to crawl around on all fours, covered in cat-skins.[80] They could watch a burlesque, with men playing the women's parts and women playing the men: quite literally a travesty of classical romantic stories.[81] Or they could view the play *The Corsican Brothers*, with men assuming female roles so effectively that Munby 'could not believe them men'.[82]

Nor should we underestimate the gender ambiguities involved with these disordered bodies. The acrobat M'lle Lulu (see illus. 81), billed by the press as a 'beautiful and courageous young lady', was, it later transpired, a man. Munby saw Lulu at the Holborn Amphitheatre in 1871, describing her as 'a small and slight but well made girl of 18 or 20, French looking ... and very pretty'. Seven years later, doctors revealed that 'she' was a he. Lulu was still performing in the 1880s, but with short hair and a resplendent moustache.[83]

Chris Straayer has analyzed the interplay of gender in what she has termed the temporary transvestite film.[84] A distinction is sometimes drawn between transvestism and cross-dressing. The transvestite's goal is to pass as the opposite sex: to trick the perception of the viewer. The cross-dresser, on the other hand, either through exaggerated parading of the attributes of the opposite sex, or due to the retention of unambiguous marks of gender, does not fool the viewer: he or she is obviously a man or woman in disguise. Straayer's argument is that the temporary transvestite film involves both types of masquerade: other characters in the film are tricked (transvestism), but the audience are not (cross-dressing). The result is

a field in which visual language conventions are strained by the use of known actors, ideological patterns, gender clichés, and sexual stereotypes to reveal as well as to disguise sex. Juxtapositions repeatedly violate the semiotic system that naturalizes sex-typed society. This play of visual signifiers keeps gender constructions shifting and produces an image of sex and gender that is often surreal.[85]

If we remove the well-known actors from the scenario, Straayer's analysis could be a description of what occurs in Munby's representa-

63, 64 Press images of pitwomen from the 1870s: The upper one is from the *Graphic*'s coverage of the South Wales colliers' strike (1873); the lower one is from an article on the Wigan colliery girls in *Pictorial World* (1874). *Pictorial World* wrote of the women's babies brought to them during their dinner-hour: 'There is something very strange in the picture of these black, masculine-looking creatures in trousers and clogs with brass tips, hugging their white-faced babies among the coals. While our artist was sketching he was the object of much jesting and fun.'

tions. He is the script-writer, director, artistic director, director of photography, producer and one of the actors, while we (his readers) are the audience before which he parades his hybrids. It is true that it is really a private showing; the 'film' is for Munby's use, and we are uninvited onlookers, voyeurs of the arch-voyeur. Our culture is an almost insurmountable barrier to reading the images that Munby provides. Familiar with the female penis and the male vagina, apprised of female masculinity, aware of a post-modern moment when young women wearing trousers under their dresses was a statement of chic, it is extremely difficult to recapture the shock of Munby's representations. And yet it is possible to see that (as in Straayer's films) something unsettling is occurring. Gender ambiguity, fluidity, contradiction and trickery are there at every turn.

This inability to decide is the hallmark of transvestism/cross-dressing (to collapse the categories for a moment) where the categories of male and female are disrupted. As Marjorie Garber has explained, 'If transvestism offers a critique of binary sex and gender distinctions, it is not because it simply makes such distinctions reversible but because it denaturalises, destabilizes, and defamiliarizes sex and gender *signs*.' Many people when confronted with cross-dressing or transvestism (Garber points out) look through it for the man or woman underneath. But another way to read transvestism is to look at the surface – at what is represented – something neither male or female. It is the 'dislocation' and 'difference' that provide the erotic charge in transvestism, which always involves both the dresser and the viewer.[86] The essence of transvestism, as one perceptive novelist has put it, is 'the coexistence, in a single body, of masculine and feminine signifiers: the tension, the repulsion, the antagonism which is created between them'.[87] The other significance of transvestism, to bring us back to the start of this chapter, is its artifice, its constructed nature. It shows that ordinary maleness and femaleness are also constructed, and thereby highlights the artificiality of gendering.

I have invoked the work of Garber and Straayer, but perhaps the most appropriate recent comparison is Judith Halberstam's study of what she has termed female masculinity, the worlds of the drag kings who perform masculinity, the drag butches who live their masculinity, and the gender-ambiguous bodies in the art of Del Grace and Catherine Opie – bearded and tattooed dykes and 'gender-unreadable' photographs of bodies. Halberstam's book, which contains images of her own masculinity, not only demonstrates gender diversity and instability and the multiplicity of masculinity, but establishes a powerful case for the inherence of masculinity in the female body, 'for the multiple ways in which women produce and name new masculinities'. Halberstam begins and ends her book with a striking representation of a bull dyke. The painting, by Sadie Lee, is called *Raging Bull* (illus. 65):

The painting confronts us with the hard stare of a bull dyke, a powerful and built body that is not obviously female but that is obviously not male. The face has no facial hair, and the chest gives a hint of bound breasts. The bull dyke's arms are folded in defiance, and they are disproportionately large for the body. The raging bull wears butch drag, the white T-shirt, blue jeans, and black belt, and the red backdrop reflects the rage in the bull dyke's eyes. Like the portraits of alternately gendered bodies by Del Grace and Cathy Opie, this image challenges the viewer by staring straight out from the canvas and fixing the viewer within the butch's gaze. The butch resists the position of becoming an object of scrutiny and returns the stare with hard resolve.[88]

The female masculinity in this painting lies in the clothing, exaggerated limbs, posture and gaze. The languages of Halberstam's delineation also reinforce it: 'powerful', 'defiance', 'large', 'rage', 'hard resolve'. This is a lesbian aesthetic, not transportable to the nineteenth-century working-class images that we have been considering. And yet the bull dyke's signs of female masculinity are not poles apart from the masculine women of Munby's fantasies (compare illus. 66). When Halberstam discusses the possibility of nineteenth-century female masculinity, she focuses on same-sex erotic attraction, particularly the famous case of Anne Lister. Munby's women would have provided a much more nuanced and challenging historical – and 'heterosexual' – counterpoint to the mixing of codes that Halberstam demonstrates for the late twentieth century.[89]

Of course, Munby's women, apart from the passing males (the cross-dressers), were not inventing their masculinities. We have been dealing with representations, not identities. This is not to say that such identities did not exist; the pitwomen talked about one another as being 'like a mon' or 'like a great lad'.[90] But this chapter has been concerned more with surfaces. I have fastened on the way in which Munby's representations are of hybrids; even the cross-dressers have elements of hybridity – witness the 'strong lad in petticoats' who was biologically a woman.

This disordering of gender was achieved through a complex mix of representations of bodies and dress. Bodies were both revealed and hidden by cross-sexed clothing as the anticipations and codes of gender were thwarted at every glance. Ironically, it was the unveiled body of the acrobat which provided one of the most powerful mask-

65 Female masculinity, 1994: Sadie Lee, *Raging Bull.*

66 Female masculinity, 1870: Jane Brown, collier.

ings of sexual difference – 'I have never seen a more complete abnegation of sex.' Disruptions of womanliness were signified in multiple
ways: hair (short), bodily size (height, width, largeness of shoulders,
arms, legs, feet, hands, neck, waist), voice (roughness), skin colour and
texture (black, sunburnt, rough), clothing (coarse, heavy, bulky:
trousers and coats) and general demeanour (gestures, strides, muscularity and posture – folded arms, for example). Such were signifiers of
the manly woman. But these manlike or masculine signifiers never
existed without their 'other', the feminine. Femininity was proclaimed
in the girlish voice, blue eyes, rosy cheeks, soft hair, pouting lips,
blushing skin and childlike demeanour, and in comeliness, delicacy,
prettiness, purity, innocence, gentleness and girlishness.

Sometimes, it was the contrast between separate bodies which
established the disruptions. Thus we have the square, ill-shaped,
horny and *masculine* woman's hand, and the tender, rose-white, delicate, soft, translucent, *feminine* hand of a man. But more often, it was
the incongruity to be found in the same body which produced
Munby's 'sexless creatures'. It was the combination of signs that
produced the powerful hybridity: the pretty face with the monstrous

68 Hannah Cullwick as a man: It is interesting that her hands are hidden, presumably because they would have been too big for those of a cultured man.

hand; the girlish head with muscular legs and arms; women in trousers who sang like angels; womanly beauty beneath the soot; and the woman's heart under a man's waistcoat.

Finally, we should recall that Munby married one of his hybrids, his servant/wife Hannah Cullwick. He celebrated her feats of physical strength (illus. 67), recording her bodily dimensions: height, weight, girth around neck, waist, biceps (her right upper arm was thicker than her neck), wrist, the breadth of her hand (he had crossed out 'hoof'). He noted that she wore men's-sized boots and gloves.[91] When she was a servant, she cropped her hair (hidden from her employers under her servant's cap) and kept it cut close for a year or more, 'as short as a man's', wearing it like that for Munby; it added 'one more to the outward contrast between her and fine ladyhood, & so I like it'.[92] In 1862, when they discussed going away together on holiday and Munby thought it impossible that she could go with him dressed either as a servant or as a lady (her class would still show through her clothing), Cullwick suggested something which Munby confessed he had been contemplating: she could go with him 'in men's clothes!' (illus. 68).[93] Cullwick had the hands of a servant, but the face of a lady; her 'fair pure body' beneath her clothes contrasted with her 'robust round arms and roughened hands'.[94]

The irony is that while Munby's imagery disorders boundaries and bodies – and we, the readers or viewers, appreciate this dissolution – authorial (directorial) intent was probably the opposite, a fetishized endorsement of the subverted ideal: true Victorian femininity.

5 Dorothy's Hands: Feminizing Men

I

An entry in Arthur Munby's diaries records an imagined encounter between a passing gang of dustwomen and the leisured occupants of a London park. Munby was tantalized by the contrast between the dustwomen and the upper-class patrons, and fantasized about paying one of the gang to bring these social poles into sharp collision: '… give one of the brawny black lasses a shilling, send her into the midst of the lounging perfumed swells, and note the effect.'[1] It was 'about as good an instance of social differences as one could have. Two women are brought face to face here: and the fact that one is a duchess & the other a dustwoman is obviously of far more value than the prior fact that both are women'. However, he found it even more instructive to make cross-sex comparisons:

Here, for instance, is a lithe languid youth, seated among his fellows on the chairs: he is immaculate, gorgeous in wellfitting raiment; his small feet are cased in bright boots, his white slender hands are shielded by gloves of delicate tint, that never knew a stain: he is not necessarily effeminate, yet sweet odours hang about him, and all his gestures are refined & courtly.

Close past him, with long strides, walks a young woman, as tall as he is and twice as broadly built: her clothes are rough, ragged, and soiled; her voice is loud & her gestures uncouth and masculine; her face and hands – the latter twice as large and strong as his – are bare and blackened; they are a deep redbrown in colour, and in texture, coarse and weatherstained: his, we know, are fair & delicate, almost, as a child … Is it not obvious that difference of sex is as nothing, in presence of so great a difference on the other side, in aspect, manners, character?[2]

I have argued repeatedly in this book that the reinforced 'other' in Munby's bodily disruptions was female, the Victorian ideal of femininity. In the previous chapter, we examined the various markers of a type of hybrid female masculinity inscribed on the bodies of working women. But what if there is a double reinforcement at work in

Munby's fantastic representations: a masculine other? For the shattering of the attributes and expectations of femininity had obvious ramifications for the masculinity of the male observer. When the broadly built young dustwoman passed the slender young man, he was feminized at the point of her masculinization. Indeed, we encountered the feminizing of men through the masculinizing of women in the sketches and descriptions of the previous chapter: the huge-handed, big-booted working women, and the small-handed, tiny-shoed gentlemen. The 'abnegation of sex' of acrobatic performance which Munby detected involved the gender ambiguity of the male as well as the female performer.

The possibilities of such spectacular inversion are captured most tellingly in that famous work of *fin-de-siècle* literature, J. K. Huysmans' *À Rebours* ('Against the Grain') of 1884. Like Munby, the hero of *À Rebours*, the Duc Jean des Esseintes, was attracted to female acrobats, describing much the same feelings of gender inversion at the moment of scrutiny. As he watched Miss Urania, an acrobat with 'a supple figure, sinewy legs, muscles of steel, arms of iron', his mind

filled with strange notions. The more he admired her strength and suppleness, the more he seemed to see an artificial change of sex operating in her; her pretty allurements, her feminine affectations fell more and more into the background, while in their stead were developed the charms attaching to the agility and vigour of a male. In a word, after being a woman to begin with, then something like an androgyne, she now seemed to become definitely and decisively and entirely a man.

But it was a double transformation, for

he presently arrived at the conclusion that, on his side, he was himself getting nearer and nearer the female type. This point reached, he was seized with a definite desire to possess this woman, craving for her as an anaemic young girl will for some great, rough Hercules whose arms can crush her to jelly in their embrace.

In other words, the moment witnessed a 'change of sex between Urania and himself'.[3]

We can recall similar moments for Munby – and not merely with acrobats (illus. 69):

We read in novels, how the highborn hero receives in his broad palm the little white hand of his rustic love: well, here is the rustic maiden & here the big bearded hero – and lo, *his* is the 'small white' hand, and *hers* the big broad palm which his comparatively slender fingers span with difficulty.[4]

Genders were reversed as Munby shook hands with the servant Elizabeth Shepstone: 'I grasped that large lump of splintered horn that

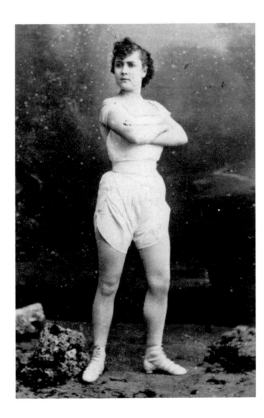

69 Gender inversion at the point of scrutiny: Ada Menken, 1868.

scratched and pierced my own hand with its pressure.'[5] Munby's poem *Ann Morgan's Love* lingers interestingly on gender inversion as the man becomes the maid and the maid a man:

> Look at mah Master, then, an' look at me!
> Wi' his fine fingers an' his dainty ways
> He's like a laady; an' Ah often thinks
> He is a laady, when Ah waits on him –
> An' me a common mon.[6]

Hands were one of Munby's special fetishes (illus. 70–76). At a dinner in the early 1860s, he contrasted the delicate hands of the gentlemen with the huge hands of a female servant:

Think of the varied beauty and meanings of a human hand: graceful and slender in outline, lithe and supple in use, delicate in substance, half transparent against the light; its framework of slight bone and its broidery of blue veins showing plain through the tender rose-white skin along the back and fingers; and the sensitive palm glowing with shell pink tints, and charming with a leaf-like delicateness of soft surface lines and swelling curves. And then think of a hand which has lost, or never had, these graces; whose characteristics are the very opposite of these. This servant wench, for instance:

her hands are large out of all proportion, square, illshaped, masculine: the broad palms are coated thick with added layers of leathery skin, of a deep yellow-brown hue; they are clammy to the touch, yet smooth and polished by work so that all the delicate skin lines are effaced, and only a few deep folds left – deep and coarse as the folds in a bull's neck; sense of feeling is all but gone from her palm and her thickened fingers. On the backs of her hands and fingers, too, not a trace of their normal character is visible: bones and blue veins, and all the exquisite modulations of form and colour, are over-grown by and hidden for ever under a monstrous expanse of coarse red hide, rough and unseemly to sight and touch, & reticulated all over with rude cracks, which have taken the place of the tender microscopic lines that beautify the natural skin. Such a hand can never be clean, nor sweetsavoured: and even if it could, what must be the result to a woman (for to a man, mind you, the result is small) of carrying about with her always, instead of a true human hand, such a brutal excrescence as this?[7]

Hands fascinated Munby because (with the face) they were the 'outward pride' of women. He thought that the awkwardness of the hands of working women made them humble, which to him was a virtue. 'My theory is that the hands and person, but not the self, of a working woman *ought* to be coarse.'[8]

Some of Munby's friends were aware of his preoccupation with large hands.[9] He raised the subject of his interest with John Ruskin in

71, 72 Factory hands:
factory worker,
Manchester, 1865
(author's close-up below).

73, 74 Servant hands: country
servant girl, aged about 24,
Westminster Road, 1862
(author's close-up below).
'She had come to London to see
the Exhibition. Her hands were
very large, coarse, and red, as if
she'd done rare hard work: and
she seemed *proud* of them…'

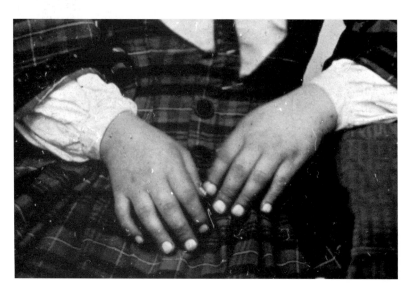

75, 76 Unidentified hands: anonymous woman and baby (author's close-up below).

1859, when he was viewing the latter's collection of paintings by J.M.W. Turner and William Henry Hunt. He told Ruskin that some-one should

paint peasant girls & servant maids as they are – coarse & hearty & homely – and so shame the false whitehanded wenches of modern art. *These* have been painted as they are, but *women*, never: spurious refinement & false delicacy prevent it – as if a housemaid was not as well worth painting as a lady – & as if, being painted, she ought to be idealised & varnished with the halfgentility of a lady's maid![10]

Munby's diaries are filled with observations about servants' hands. There is his surprisingly modern-sounding disquisition on class and sex, provoked by the sight of a servant's hands as she waited on him and his friends:

Now, though her hands were larger than those of the three men at table – though they were much coarser in texture, much ruder in tint – was she any the less feminine for that? Are the relations of the sexes really inverted, when three men sit at table, with hands delicate & jewelled, and a woman stands behind and waits, offering the dishes with a large coarse hand that makes her master's look almost ladylike? And is it the proper thing, that the *women* should sit, as at a ball supper, drawing the gloves from their dainty fingers, and waited upon by *men*, whose hands, that seemed so ladylike by comparison with Molly's, look sinewy and laborious by the side of Blanch's tender tips? If *this* is right for one class, is *that* for the other? In short, what, in the Equation of Life, is the respective value of the terms *sex* and *station*?[11]

In 1862, Munby glimpsed the thumb of a servant momentarily side-by-side with that of a lady as she steadied a plate. His mind photographed the fractional encounter – thick red against slender white – for a later sketch to accompany a journal entry: '... besides the intense opposition of colour, the thumb of the maid servant was at least four times as big as that of the lady.' Then, he manoeuvred his own hand next to that of the servant. It was, he wrote, half the size of hers, and quite 'white and ladylike' in comparison. The hands of the servant were bigger than those of any of the men in the room, and 'infinitely more masculine in colour and texture'.[12]

Of the various body parts, the hand features more than most in Munby's descriptions of slipping masculinity. In the imagined encounter between the dustwoman and the languid youth, the perfumed park lounger has slender white hands: the hands of the woman are twice as large and strong. Munby compared his own hands with those of a milkwoman:

... it was the hand of a slight girl to that of a big man of low class: only *hers* was the man's. Absurd contrast! I, a bearded man of more than average height & bulk; she, a woman, still young, and scarcely so tall as my shoulder: and yet, without hyperbole or self-flattery, my hand was white and small and frail-looking as a lady's beside that thick and clumsy mass.[13]

One of the great contrasts that Munby so enjoyed in his relationship with Hannah was 'between her large hardworking hands and his hands'.[14] My argument in this chapter is that the metonymic and synecdochic hand assumed huge significance in this other 'othering'.

To grasp (so to speak) Munby's obsession with hands, we need to return to the philosophy of physiognomy, discussed in the earlier chapter on noses. Like the face, the hand was particularly important as an indicator of class and refinement. Joseph Simms devoted several pages to the handshake, making it clear that – as Munby well knew – the touching of hands was a means of revealing character. The 'soul' was declared in the hand as well as in the face.[15] As we have also seen, Mary Cowling has highlighted the attention paid to aristocratic phys- iognomy in Frith's *Derby Day*; this detail included hands as well as faces (see illus. 27): 'The ungloved hand of the right-hand gentleman is smooth, with long, curving fingers, and finely shaped oval nails.'[16] The logic dictated a hierarchy, shading into the animal; in the sketched outlines of hands provided in *The Psychonomy of the Hand* (1865), the gorilla is placed close to the tracing of the 'spatulous' hand of the 'English Navvy'.[17] The smaller the hand, the more refined its owner. Largeness of hand, particularly of palm, indicated brutishness and lack of delicacy. Munby represented Elizabeth Shepstone's hands as hooves, the paws of a beast: 'Is this a hand? Is this a human hand?' Unable to bend them properly, she could not sew, knit or even make a bed, for they would have torn the sheets. She could barely handle a knife and fork. But she could spend days on her hands and knees, scrubbing.[18] Munby's descriptions of the domestic servant linger on so-called hoofing: crevices, shavings and lumps. When he gave Shep- stone a shilling, it stuck (surely it was wishful thinking) in one of the cracks of her hand![19]

We may recall that Hannah Cullwick's hands declared her humble calling (illus. 77); she would hold them out so that potential employ- ers could see this physical declaration of hard labour. They were her reference or curriculum vitae. The hands of Shepstone likewise were testimonials to her hard work, 'reading there / The history of a strong laborious life'.[20] Hands were a badge of occupation and class. There is a passage in Thomas Hardy's *Hand of Ethelberta* about the hand of Ethelberta's brother:

… look how my thumb stands out at the root, as if it were out of joint, and that hard place inside there. Did you ever see anything so ugly as that hand – a misshaped monster, isn't he? That comes from the jack-plane, and my pushing against it day after day and year after year. If I were found drowned or buried, dressed or undressed, in fustian or in broadcloth, folk would look at my hand and say, 'that man's a carpenter.'[21]

77 Hannah's hand: author's close-up from the original photograph (see illus. 34).

As has already been intimated, hands were also a declaration of femininity. As with the nose, the female hand is almost an after-thought in the heavily gendered physiognomic texts. It is not until Chapter 18 of *Psychonomy of the Hand* that discussion shifts to women: 'It only remains to speak of the Female Hand, before we take leave of a subject replete with interest ...' Again – another parallel with the reading of faces – less is better. Small hands and long (less knotted) fingers indicated an intuitive rather than reasoned morality. The delicacy of the 'female hand' represented woman's aversion to 'scientific, political or moral investigations', and freedom from 'all the restraints which the laws of deduction and of logic impose': 'While she trusts her instincts she is scarcely ever deceived, but she is gener-ally lost when she begins to reason.' Her moral superiority, tenderness and 'greater delicacy of perception' were, like the shape of her hands, the natural inheritance of her sex![22]

But hands have one further significance. The hand, William Cohen has reminded us, 'is the only exposed site of sexual communication below the neck'.[23] While his rather notorious account of the deployment of Victorian sexuality in the novels of Charles Dickens focuses on masturbation (Charley Bates: 'Master Bates': masturbates!), it is an interesting demonstration of the importance of the hand 'both as a site of sexual signification and as a dangerous sexual implement'.[24] Nor is sexual communication limited to the nineteenth century; one of Hannah Cullwick's most recent historians has declared her erotic attraction to Munby's picture of his servant/wife's hardened hands: 'Why are Hannah's hands so sexual to me?'[25]

III

There is a subplot in an episode of the television comedy series *Seinfeld* in which George Costanza finally becomes an object of desire when a hand-modelling agent discovers his hands. During the photo session, a 'great-looking girl' (George's description) makes a play for him ('Your hands are beautiful') and provides her phone number. George skips back from his assignment – hands in the air – in anticipation of future delights. However, as the hardened viewer would have anticipated, George will never get to capitalize on his new-found sexual attraction. The subplot intersects with the main story – Jerry and the others are engaged in the Puffy Shirt denouement – and George Costanza, hand model, burns his assets on an iron which Kramer has left on. The fantasy of sexual excess vanishes: the soft, sexy hands become burnt, bandaged hands. The episode also contains a hilarious warning about the dangers of self-abuse in the apocryphal tale of George's predecessor, the hand model Ray McKigney: 'He could've had any woman in the world ... but none could match the beauty of his own hand ... and that became his own true love.' Ray fell victim to auto-eroticism; muscular spasm set in through overuse, and the 'soft and milky white', perfectly formed hand degenerated into a claw (he 'was dependent on Cub Scouts to feed him'). 'You are his successor. [George looks down at his hands.] I only hope you have a little more self-control.'[26]

In this slice of late twentieth-century life, the hand is a sexual object. Even Kramer sees George in a new light: 'Let's see ... oh, those are nice. You know, I've never noticed this before! They're smooth ... creamy ... delicate, yet [turns to Jerry] masculine.' Kramer's 'yet masculine' is all-important. George's hands have the attributes of femininity, but his masculinity is not compromised: they literally hold untold (heterosexual) promise: '... this great looking girl gave me her phone number ... I got it! I got it all! I'm busting. Jerry, I'm busting!'[27]

So, can we move the argument about the significance of Munby's feminized hands up a notch? Did the feminization of masculinity referred to earlier have implications for sexual signification?

The slender hand is certainly a recurring trope in representations of othered sexuality and gender in the late nineteenth and early twentieth centuries. Let us start with Oscar Wilde's *The Picture of Dorian Gray*, which has acquired iconic status in the history of male homosexuality. Indeed, Cohen's observation about the importance of hands in Dickens could equally be made of Wilde. Hands are invoked at every turn of the page in *Dorian Gray*. Sometimes, they convey intimacy between man and woman: Dorian's beloved Sibyl kisses his hands, stroking his hair with her 'little fingers', pressing his hands to her lips, putting her hand on his arm; the mere touch of her hand makes him forget the dandy, Lord Henry. But hands also show intimacy between men: Dorian and Lord Henry are continually touching one another on the arm or shoulder. Hands represent rejection ('Don't touch me!') as well as desperation ('Her little hands stretched blindly out').[28]

Lord Henry has Pygmalion-like aspirations for Dorian: talking to him is like 'playing upon an exquisite violin'. He wants to shape him: 'There was nothing that one could not do with him.' So, hands signify control too. They also represent old age and decay. Hence when Dorian compares his own ageless beauty with the corrupt visage of his portrait, the picture of Dorian Gray, 'the evil and aging face on the canvas' and the 'fair young face' in the mirror, he also compares the hands: 'He would place his white hands beside the coarse bloated hands of the picture, and smile.' And hands proclaim Dorian's guilt. After his killing of Basil, one of the hands in his portrait is covered with a 'loathsome red dew ... as though the canvas had sweated blood'. As the novel moves towards its climax, the blood on the hand in the portrait seems brighter, has dripped onto the feet, and has spread to the other hand.[29]

More importantly for the purposes of this argument, hands signify a kind of aberrant sexuality. The beautiful Dorian has 'finely-chiselled nostrils' and 'cool, white, flower-like hands'. His 'delicate hands' twitch when he hungers for opium. Lord Henry has 'long fingers', 'pale, fine-pointed fingers'. The fingers of the fictional dandies stray across the piano keys and stroke an exotic parrot as they talk about marriage ('Married life is merely a habit, a bad habit') and crime and art ('I should fancy that crime was to them [the lower orders] what art is to us, simply a method of procuring extraordinary sensations').

Later, Dorian looks at his hands as at those of a murderer; 'his own white taper fingers', hands that have murdered, hold a poem by Gautier comparing *his* own smooth white hands with those of the severed hands of a murderer! Hands signify Dorian's double life, 'the terrible pleasure of a double life': 'Those finely-shaped fingers could never have clutched a knife for sin.'[30]

Above all, *The Picture of Dorian Gray* is about a feminized masculinity fastening on the delicate-handed dandy. Wilde himself was seen as effeminate; the indeterminacy of his sex and gender could be read on his body. One of the markers of his degeneracy, interestingly enough, was the largeness of his nose. Another was his limp hands. Wilde's 'fleshly indulgence and laziness ... were written all over him', according to Frank Harris. 'He shook hands in a limp way I disliked; his hands were flabby, greasy.' The caption in a *Punch* illustration of 1892 refers to Wilde's 'daintily-gloved fingers' holding a burning cigarette. He had 'small pointed hands'.[31]

The implication, then – to return to the object of this exercise – is that there are two linked, but not identical, possibilities for the reading of Munby's feminized hands: the feminine and the queer. A number of critics have argued that Wilde's work and life stood at a pivotal point in the queering of the effeminate male. In *Dorian Gray*, the dandy was not exclusively attracted to men. Rather, he was a misogynist whose main sexual impulse was towards women, but who was also homoerotically inclined to men. Wilde and his dandies were perceived as effeminate. Alan Sinfield has explained it nicely: 'The dandy figure served Wilde's project because he had a secure cross-sex image, yet might anticipate, on occasion and in the main implicitly, an emergent same-sex identity.' The dandy was able to 'commute ... between diverse sexualities'.[32] By the end of the Wilde trials in the 1890s, the effeminate male had become more exclusively associated with same-sex erotic attraction. The Wildean moment, then, is considered important in the constituting of homosexuality. 'The supplementing of "aesthetic" effeminacy with connotations of male sexual desire for other men', writes Ed Cohen, 'is one of the consequences of the newspaper representations of the Wilde trials.'[33]

Hands, then, could clearly indicate sexual ambivalence – in both senses of the term. During the early twentieth century, hands feature in the gay sexual aesthetic recreated so skilfully by Terry Castle. Jonathan Brockett, a character in Radclyffe Hall's famous lesbian novel *The Well of Loneliness* (1928), has hands 'as white and soft as a woman's'. Noel Coward's 'womanly' white hands, 'languidly supporting a cigarette', were elemental to his style, his affected aestheticism.[34] As late as the 1940s, a study of sex variants in New York was using the hand as one of the many bodily indicators of an individual's mix of masculine and feminine traits and therefore of their sexuality. The size of a hand characterized masculinity in women (large) and femininity in men (small). Thus the male bisexual Tracy O. had 'small delicate hands' which were used to demonstrate the 'effeminacy ... evident in his general appearance, his postures, and his slightly mincing gait'. The homosexual Rodney S. had 'a sensual mouth, slender, delicate hands and well-kept fingers ... His voice is high pitched and his gait is a little mincing'. The recurring theme is of a linkage between male homosexuality and 'slender, delicate hands and ... long, tapering fingers', a descriptive combination mentioned time and time again.[35] George Costanza would be horrified.

In women in the same study, the formula is generally that large hands represent feminine masculinity.

In body type Aimee belongs to the group called boyish-feminine. She has a round face, quite broad at the level of the cheek bones, and a well-developed forehead. Her scanty eyebrows, her slightly upturned nose, her mouth and her chin give the impression of small features. Her hands are somewhat broad and her fingers a little stubby. Moreover, she lacks the usual feminine flexibility in wrist movements and in her posture and gait. Her body is short and stocky and she has heavy, well-developed shoulders which are wider than her hips. This sturdiness and rigidity are offset somewhat by well-developed breasts.

Large hands, thick wrists and an inflexibility of wrist movement are some of the indicators of female homosexuality.

'In her body form and in her activities', Patricia D. is a

composite of masculine and feminine characteristics. Casual inspection of her body form suggests the boyish feminine adolescent. Her breasts are large, the fat in her upper arms is soft, her waist is slender, and her hips are well developed. In contrast to these features are her heavy, square jaw, strong neck, large hands and feet and straight, sturdy legs.

'Her gait was masculine and there was a distinct lack of feminine flexibility in wrist movements.' As for Kathleen M., 'Probably no amount of artifice would conceal her masculine attributes. She is tall, square shouldered, flat chested, and her hips are obviously narrower than her shoulders. Strong, long-fingered hands terminate the upper extremities.'[36] The lesbian hand, Mandy Merck has written, 'has a cultural history in which it figures both as an instrument of sexual contact and as a marker of gender transitivity'.[37]

The hand, then, could easily become the homosexual hand. The memoirs of John Addington Symonds provide a Victorian example of such a process at work. Symonds was an important figure on the Victorian literary scene who later collaborated with the famous sexologist Havelock Ellis. However, the homosexual Symonds resisted the common categorization of such desires as effeminate – the female soul trapped in a male body:

Morally and intellectually, in character and taste and habits, I am more masculine than many men I know who adore women. I have no feminine feeling for the males who rouse my desire. The anomaly of my position is that I admire the physical beauty of men more than women, derive more pleasure from their contact and society, and am stirred to sexual sensations exclusively by persons of the male sex.[38]

Hands have a palpable presence in this retrospective ordering of Symonds's homosexual longings. They are etched on his developmental psyche. On his twelfth birthday, when he went to kiss his father, Symonds senior said, 'Shake hands; you are grown too old for kissing.' The hand of the father had replaced the pre-pubescent goodnight kiss. Hands also figured in Symonds's earliest sexual experiences – at the hands of the headmaster of Harrow, for example. Symonds, who eventually exposed the master for his affair with one of his students, refers to his disgust with a man from whose hands he had received the sacrament – the same hands that had stroked Symonds's thigh while the headmaster read Greek iambics to him.[39]

Symonds's first love (he was eighteen) was a chorister, Willie, a youth with slender hands. They only kissed on the lips twice in their relationship, and it took a year for Symonds to 'do more than touch his hand': 'He enabled me to realize an ideal of a passionate and yet pure love between friend and friend.' This was to become a familiar pattern in his repressed sexuality; for a significant part of his life the only sexual contact that he had with all the young men he desired was the touch of their hands.[40]

Hands were very much a part of his attraction to men, as in this diary entry for 23 March 1889, when Symonds was in his late 40s:

I have been sitting opposite a young man in the *diligence* [coach] all day – a peasant about nineteen, with a well-knit frame and good healthy face, exhibiting no special beauty but radiating intelligence and the magnetic force of the male adolescent. I looked at his hands – great powerful palms and fingers, fashioned to mould and clasp, yet finely shaped, and attached to sinewy wrists, where the skin had smoother texture, showing veins and the salience of sinews. Enough of his throat and forearms was visible to make one divine how white and wholesome was the flesh of the young man's body.

I felt I could have kissed those hands hardened with labour, bruised here and there, brown in complexion – have kissed them and have begged of them to touch me. Then it flashed across my mind that no woman's hands – whether of duchess or milkmaid, maiden or married – had ever possessed for me such sexual attraction as these of the young peasant had.[41]

Hands appear again in his description of the boy 'Norman' with whom he fell in love in 1870 – 'For there is the soul in the fingers. They speak. The body is but silent, a dumb eloquent animated work of art made by the divine artificer'; 'How his head drooped on one shoulder, and how his arm lay curved along flank and thigh, and how upon the down of dawning manhood lay his fingers, and how the shrinking god was covered by his hand.'[42]

The case study of Symonds which appears in the 'Sexual Inversion in Men' section of various editions of Ellis's *Studies in the Psychology of Sex* states that it was not until his mid- to late 30s that he 'began freely to follow homosexual inclinations'. Before that, at the height of the neurosis provoked by his sense of his sexual difference and unwillingness to indulge his homosexual longings, he contemplated compromise:

Having no passion for women, it was easy to avoid them. Yet they inspired him with no exact horror. *He used to dream of finding an exit from his painful situation by cohabitation with some coarse, boyish girl of the people*; but his dread of syphilis stood in the way.[43]

IV

Munby's poem *Dorothy*, which draws heavily on his interactions with Hannah Cullwick and other working women, deals with the courtship of a farm servant with huge hands. Hands are vital to this poem; the word *hand* occurs some 135 times in 85 pages of verse. When men kiss Dorothy's horned hands, they are instantly feminized: '... with such hands as these, just like a labouring man's! / Man's, did I say? Why, these are a many times coarser nor mine are'.

> Lightly he took her hand; intending, doubtless, to press it:
> Meaning at least to bestow some pretty compliment there;
> But, as to one in the dark, who, feeling for silk or for velvet,
> Suddenly grasps unawares rusty old iron instead,
> So did it happen to him, thus grasping the hand of our Dolly –
> Rough as old iron, and hard – terribly callous – within.
> Singular contrast, this, these two hands mated together!
> One so laborious and large, one so refined and so small;

> Singular, too, to reflect – these young folk facing each other,
> He no effeminate man, she a most womanly maid –
> Curious, I say, to reflect that the hands were not as their owners:
> That which was small and refined, slender and soft, was the man's;
> That which was clumsy and coarse, and big, was the hand of the maiden!
> *He* was the lady, it seem'd; *she* was the muscular man.

The poet's female character exclaims: 'My, what a hand his was – as soft an' as tender as satin! / What must a *lady's* be, if there's such hands in a *man?*'[44]

The exit that had tempted Symonds was displacement, what Christopher Craft has termed the transposition of the homosexual into and through the heterosexual. Craft has discovered it in the trope of the vampire, where men have sexual contact through the body of the interposing female.[45] Did Munby similarly displace deeper-lying desires? Were his attractions to working women, and *actual* cohabitation with a 'coarse, boyish girl of the people', a circuitous route to homosexuality? Do the large-handed, big-bodied women – like Craft's vampires – represent a moment, or many moments, when 'an implicitly homosexual desire achieves representation as a monstrous heterosexuality, as a demonic inversion of normal gender relations'?[46] Was *Dorothy* a conduit for the poet's lips when Mr Robert 'Kiss'd that cold grey palm, cooling his lips with the horn!' – feminine lips on masculine hands.[47] Are Munby's masculine females akin to the nineteenth-century male literary fascination with lesbianism and the masculine woman, what has been called 'the wish to be woman', the projection of male homoeroticism onto the body of the female?[48] Thaïs E. Morgan and others have considered the possibility that male-to-male desire was 'detoured' through the textual lesbian bodies of nineteenth-century literature and art. Such bodies allowed 'the male beholder-reader to enjoy a sense of liberation, releasing him from the socially constructed constraints of sex-gender role into a subjectivity that oscillates between masculinities and femininities and between hetero- and homosexualities'.[49]

But if female masculinity was a route to homosexuality for Munby, it was an extremely oblique one. His diaries contain nothing of the frank, tortured sexual histories of the sexological confessions. Moreover, his recorded statements about male and female homosexuality are hardly approving ones. The poet Swinburne, he noted of an incident at the Arts Club in 1870, 'expressed a horror of sodomy, yet *would* go on talking about it'. Swinburne declared 'an actual admiration for Lesbianism', but Munby made it clear that he felt nothing but disgust for 'it' and 'regret at what he [Swinburne] has written thereon'.[50] Several years earlier, he had discussed pederasty with Lord Houghton (Richard Monkton Milnes), 'how the ancient world was based upon it, saw nothing unnatural in it ... how the thing is *encouraged* in the Russian army, and is absolutely unknown in America' (an observation that would have puzzled Americans). Again, Munby's reactions were disapproving. He did not favour the prevailing attitudes of Victorian 'men of high genius' who admired and enjoyed (the words are Munby's) 'exquisite subtleties of lust':

Of course, as I know well, these capacities ... are a protest against respectable dullness. But, instead of striving to keep them down (and a poet should feel towards purity as a woman or truly devout man does) these men give way to them: & respectable pure readers delight in their books, knowing little of what is behind.[51]

As we will see in the next chapter, there was nothing asexual about Munby's outlook and interactions, yet the object of his preoccupation was female: Dorothy had a beautiful 'feminine face' as well as a 'labourer's hand'.

Even if one would stop short of including Arthur Munby as one of those (Tennyson, Hopkins, Swinburne) who imagined male-to-male sexuality and whose 'writing [wa]s important in the cultural construction of homosexuality in the second half of the nineteenth century', his oeuvre can be seen in terms of what Richard Dellamora has described as nineteenth-century attempts to fashion 'ways of being masculine in the world'.[52] Significantly, perhaps, when Robert Browning first read Munby's anonymous poem *Dorothy*, he thought it was written by a woman: 'From some signal exquisiteness of observation, I almost fancy the fine hand must be *feminine*: if I mistake, my blunder is one more tribute the more to a consummate male craftsman.'[53] This was a more fitting tribute than Browning could ever have imagined. Munby's import lies in the history of male femininity.

6 Sexuating Arthur

I

I want to begin this last chapter with two examples of *fin-de-siècle* sexuality.[1] Richard von Krafft-Ebing's famous sexological text *Psychopathia Sexualis* (1886) contains several hundred cases of sexual fetishism, ranging from shoe and handkerchief fetishists through to sadism and masochism. One man had over four hundred women's handkerchiefs when his house was searched; there was even a moustache fetishist. This is an astonishing catalogue of what were seen as sexual perversions. Sex is displayed in bizarre forms on every page. Case 114 involves a 24-year-old male from 'a badly tainted family'. The man, referred to as 'X', had been taught to masturbate at the age of seven by a servant-girl and had 'first experienced pleasure in these manipulations when the girl happened to touch his penis with her slippered foot'. As a consequence, 'X' became excited whenever he saw or thought of women's shoes: 'Nothing else in a woman could excite him; the thought of coitus filled him with horror. Men did not interest him in any way.' At the age of eighteen, he opened a shop, which, among other things, dealt in women's shoes: 'He was excited sexually by fitting shoes on his female patrons, or by manipulating shoes that came in for mending.' He tried to overcome his fetish. He stopped selling shoes and got married; 'He married a pretty young lady. In spite of lively erections when he thought of his wife's shoes, in attempts at cohabitation he was absolutely impotent.' The man went to see a psychiatrist, who gave him bromide and advised him to hang a shoe over his bed during coitus, 'at the same time imagining his wife to be a shoe'.[2]

My next example is a work of pornography. Walter was not his real name, but it is the only name we have for the author of a piece of Victorian erotica entitled *My Secret Life*, released in a limited print-run in the 1880s and '90s: eleven volumes and over four thousand pages of, not to put too fine a point on it, fucking. (The index to

Volume XI has over two hundred entries under that heading.)[3] As Steven Marcus has observed, the calendar that Walter operates on is 'sexual time'; his is a view of Europe 'through the eye of a penis'. At the end of the volumes, he counted up twelve hundred women whom he had fucked and another three hundred whom he had felt up: '... looking through diaries and memoranda, I find that I have had women of twenty-seven different Empires, Kingdoms or Countries, and eighty or more different nationalities, including every one in Europe except a Laplander':

God bless cunt! ... God bless it for all the sweet associations and affections it produces. This act described as filthy, and not to be alluded to, is the greatest pleasure of life. All people are constantly thinking of it. After the blessed sun, surely the cunt ought to be worshipped as the source of all human happiness. It takes and gives and is twice blessed.[4]

The reader's first reaction may be to contrast the worlds of Munby and 'X' and Walter. And yet I want to argue that our approach should be a little more complex than simple polarities. Although Munby did not masturbate into footwear or imagine that his wife was a shoe, he was a practised and varied fetishist. He could scarcely be accused of priapism, but his journals are a direct complement to those of Walter. Both men engaged young women in the street. Both had dealings with many (many) servants. Both used their class position and money to buy what they wanted: in Munby's case, it was information, while in Walter's it was uncomplicated penetration. Both produced what Marcus has termed dramatized memory, taking pleasure in both the writing and the later reading of the interactions which their manuscripts inscribe.[5] Clearly, any account of Victorian sexuality has to apprehend someone like Munby, who, as we shall see, did not seem to have had sexual intercourse with anyone – including his wife – and a predator like Walter, who constantly engaged in extramarital sex, often with prostitutes, and thought of nothing else. Even if, as seems most likely, *My Secret Life* is a work of erotic fiction rather than autobiography, my point about contrasting and complementing sexual expression remains.[6]

II
We have seen manifestations of Munby's sexuality almost at every turn. Take his sketches (illus. 78) and descriptions of the female mudlarks, foraging in the river between barges, young women with their skirts wrapped tight between their legs and their thighs exposed,

78 Shock of surprise: a
mudlark, 1855.

and in the mud up to their hips; a descriptive triptych of filth (mud),
naked flesh and hard and degrading labour. Bargemen are placed to
intensify the scene of degradation by throwing food scraps to the
working women. Munby watches others watching. In one passage, he
has a bargee leaning over the edge of his barge, watching while a
mudlark, 'bare thighs visible', dislodges some bilge water and lets 'the
foul liquid spurt through the hole upon her limbs': 'I recollect the
shock of surprise which this scene gave me.'[7]

Munby was always aware of a sexual edge in his interactions with
young working women (illus. 79), the danger that these women ran in
being so open with the gentleman who struck up an acquaintance.[8] He
said as much when he recorded his interviewing of a milliner (he
thought the morality of milliners 'lower than that of any other'):
'Here was a young woman sitting in her bedroom for a whole evening,
alone with a man!' In such scenarios, he suggested, the woman's fate
lay with the man's 'responsibility'. And he obviously derived feelings
of power from such situations. He described these interactions as
having 'just enough sexual consciousness to make it romantic without

being unsafe'.[9] There are similar sexual undercurrents in his melo-dramatic description of the meeting with the servant Mary Ann Bungey, who approached him in the street to ask him for directions: 'Handsome and wholesome & fresh – just the sort of girl to attract an evildoer: and she, all alone in her simplicity, puts herself thus into the hands of a strange gentleman, near the Haymarket!' He offered to show her the way: 'Suppose my offer had been insincere: she would have accepted it all the same, and might have been decoyed into a brothel unawares.'[10] When talking about a West Country servant, he also referred to the sexual danger of the city. The woman's father kept writing to her to remind her of the immoralities of London, 'and thus, for she was an honest girl, her manly reliance on her own strength and wit was tempered by a vague fear of evil.'[11] London was indeed a city of dreadful delight.[12]

There was a clear sexual component to such cross-class interactions. The West Country servant was particularly mindful of her place: 'I am only a servant you see Sir; and you are so much better than me!' Where the modern reader may well detect a hint of irony, a not-so-hidden transcript of resistance in an overdone obsequiousness, Munby saw only temptation. He referred to the 'dangerous pathos in such words: a dangerous attractiveness in such simple incense, simply offered by the coarsest woman'. He reassured the reader (himself?) that he put these investigations on a respectable footing.[13]

There are similar elements in his photographs – if not in his mind, then at least in the understanding of those involved. After Munby had arranged for the posing of a Bermondsey dustwoman, the photographer's doorman procured a young envelope-maker who was quite prepared, for a fee, to 'have a picture of her taken *with her clothes up*'. Munby was then approached by another man who asked him if he wanted 'any ballet girls or poses plastiques?' Munby was aware that his interest in dustwomen might be perceived as a rather curious breach of taste, but he was not prepared for the blatant sexualization of these transactions: 'I thanked him coldly, and so got away at last; wondering why on earth a dustwoman's portrait should have produced these offensive results.'[14]

The most obvious example of the sexuality of the streets is revealed in Munby's story of a woman he met one night near his home at the Inner Temple. As he put it, he found her friendliness very tempting: 'I had much ado to restrain my own passions and hers.' He encountered her again, and she told him that she had prostituted herself the very evening of their last meeting 'out of mere excitement caused by her interview with me. "Didn't you see", she said, "that that was what I wanted?"' The next time he saw her, several years later, she was indeed a Regent Street prostitute. The truth of the account and Munby's assumptions about prostitution are of no consequence; what is important is that for him such encounters were potential sites of desire.[15]

Although he passed prostitutes as a matter of course – he recorded being accosted by no fewer than six one Saturday night in Ramsgate – Munby rarely engaged in conversation with them unless they were different in some way.[16] He recorded one such interaction in the Mall: '... this one was so different from the rest that I stopped & spoke to her.' She told him that she was a country girl who had been seduced by her master, and that she would be walking the streets until she died. Munby was attracted by the contrast between her wholesome appearance and the coarseness of her trade. As ever, the pathos of her situation moved him: 'I suddenly kissed her cheek: her prostitute cheek, where lustful mercenary kisses are nightly laid. Somehow, she reminded me of de Quincey's Ann.'[17] Munby was immediately confronted by a further contrast. One of the regular 'park-women' seized him by the arm and made a proposal 'so loathsome & unheard of that I felt myself growing dizzy with the thought of it'.[18] The earlier reference to Thomas de Quincey's Ann is significant, for the Opium Eater's romanticized relationship with the prostitute – the *flâneur*, a male walker of the streets, drawn naturally to a female of the streets – did not involve actual sexual intercourse, and it also featured an innocent kiss.[19] Munby moved uneasily, dizzily, though with obvious titillation, through London's erotic neighbourhoods.

His descriptions unsettle surface views of Victorian culture. When watching the performance of some male and female black-face minstrels in a London street, he was approached by one of the men, who quietly offered him a private showing ('I can provide plenty of other women besides this one'). The man said that they would dance 'and go through all the scenes of plantation life; but (lowering his voice) we cannot do these things in the street, you know Sir'. The implication was that there were two performances: one for the streets and one (not fit for public consumption) for private connoisseurs. This is further proof of the sexuality of the streets, but it also adds another dimension to black-face performance rarely discussed in its burgeoning historiography: the erotic charge of gendered racial crossings.[20]

High or low, the venues of cultural display and interaction were merely stages for the dramatic representation of Munby's desires. We have already encountered the sexual component to his fascination with female acrobats. When he saw the female acrobat de Glorion at the Oxford Music Hall in 1870, what attracted him was the way in which her top half was dressed as a woman – 'the "body" of an elegant evening dress, with roses and ribbons and a fair lawn bodice, and ornament on her throat and hair' – but as the eye traversed downwards, it was as if the bottom of her gown had been ripped away: '... instead of the decent skirts which the eye was thus led to expect, there was *nothing*: she was to all appearance naked, from the hips downward; except her boots.' He captured the image in a sketch (illus. 80). The erotic charge of female acrobatics is clear from his descriptions juxtaposed against his photographs (illus. 81–4): the woman's relative state of undress in a public arena; her physical contortions and raw strength; the displayed intermingling of male and female bodies; the parading and then shattering of perceptions of female vulnerability ('perched up there, naked and unprotected, with no one to help her ... if she had not been an acrobat, every man present would have rushed to rescue or assist her'). Although Munby was aware that other spectators may have watched the proceedings more innocently, he considered the performance to be highly sexual,

80 At the music hall, 1870: 'To all appearance naked, from the hips downward'.

the woman wrapping her naked thighs around the body of her partner, 'the familiar interlacing of male and female bodies in sight of the public'. It was, he wrote, 'gross and corrupting'. Yet he returned to watch female acrobats and provided a voyeuristic description of de Glorion which paraded several of his fetishes:

Tonight, when the girl was sitting on the trapeze with her comrades, resting a moment after having climbed up there again from the grip of their hands or feet, she observed that one of their shoes had left a stain of dust on her pink thigh. And she called his attention to it, and wetted her handkerchief and wiped the place; just as nonchalant as if she had been in her own dressing room, and not there, aloft and under the gaze of several hundred people.

Here, in a brief few words, we have the dirty imprint of foot on thigh, the all-important drawing of attention before the removal of the mark with spittle, and all before the fictive gaze of several hundred voyeurs observing a private act performed in public.[21]

But the occasion for sexualization equally could have been a visit to the stage or opera (illus. 85–6). Munby went annually to see *Fidelio*,

81–4 Bodies displayed: female
acrobats (from upper left: Lulu, 1871;
Azella, 1868; Zazel, 'The Human
Cannon Ball'; Mme. Senyah, 1868).

85 Sexual fascination: photograph of Miss Murray, actress. 'Comparing the face with the posture, this picture seems to me the most disgusting example of self degradation in a woman that I have met with.' Nonetheless, Munby bought the photo in 1869 to add to his collection.

Beethoven's only opera, attracted by the theme of female devotion and its powerful female (cross-dressed) central character. Munby referred to 'the divine prison scene', in which Leonore, wife of the imprisoned Florestan, casts off her male disguise and throws herself between her husband and his would-be assassin – 'and all along, the thought of Hannah and her noble devotion was present to me, as usual.'[22] Leonore had what for Munby was a perfect combination of power and self-sacrificing marital loyalty. But she was also a woman who appeared as a man for most of the opera.[23] (A female character even falls in love with her/him.) As with the female acrobats, male dress revealed female limbs (Leonore's legs).[24] And the iconography of chains in *Fidelio* must have reminded him of Hannah's slavery; it would have been impossible for him to remain detached from lines such as Leonore's 'for great reward love can bear even great suffering.'[25] Once, he took Cullwick to hear *Fidelio*, and they sat in the front row of the amphitheatre. Munby claimed that the sight of Hannah's hand resting on 'the cushioned balustrade', a 'large rough red hand, red as the cushion itself', caused a 'sensation' among the middle-class ladies around them. In cases like this, it is difficult to work out where

86 Watching the audience: 'Faces I saw from my stall', illustration from *London Society* (1879).

the real performance was for Cullwick and Munby: on the stage or in the audience.[26] A recent commentator has warned modern critics from reading too much into the gender ambiguity and transvestism of the opera. Beethoven, it is argued, was a 'profoundly unsexual artist': 'His art was desexualised on principle.'[27] We may recall that similar things have been said of Munby.

III

It is likely that Cullwick and Munby's relationship did not involve sexual intercourse, but it would be mistaken to describe it as non-sexual. It was extremely sexualized in the sense that sexuality always involves power and desire: '... the blacker I get with work, the more ardent I feel towards you!' Cullwick reputedly told Munby in 1874.[28] Indeed, the voyeurism and role-playing which formed such a central part of their relationship is inexplicable outside the compass of sexual interaction. Although Cullwick resisted his advances, her relationship with Munby's neighbour Thornbury was sexually charged

– not the least in her husband's recounting of it: "'Oh dear, Sir, my hand is black, an' its soiled yourn!' Whereon, she told me, "I wetted the corner o' my apron wi' my lips, & wiped his hand; an' he let me do it!'"[29]

Cullwick and Munby's sleeping arrangements are unclear and varied according to the various phases of their relationship. They slept separately before marriage and for much of their married life, but did sleep in the same bed sometimes.[30] It is almost certain that they did not have sexual intercourse before marriage; in 1860, Munby described Cullwick's love for him as 'a mother's love'.[31] When Cullwick stayed overnight with him at his house in 1860 for the first time – something he termed a 'dangerous experiment' – he noted in his diary that it was temptation overcome: 'I learnt somewhat of physical temptation and of resistance.' They slept separately that night. There is pointed reference to Hannah's 'virgin sleep'.[32] In 1862, Munby referred to 'the temptation of last time', temptation overcome, and how he was able to kiss her 'with due self control' as she lay 'alone' in his spare bed.[33] One of Cullwick's letters in 1870 describes Munby as being 'virtuous, & in every respect a gentleman'.[34] When they went to Southend together in 1872, they had two bedrooms.[35] In 1893, reminiscing about their early years, Munby wrote that when she visited his rooms during their long courtship, her only safeguards were 'his honour and her own powerful frame and pure resolve'.[36] Historians have claimed that the regime of continence continued after marriage – and Cullwick's description of their love as '*pure*' lends support to this theory.[37] As in the novels of R. D. Blackmore, a friend with whose work Munby and Cullwick were familiar, sexual self-control was a mark of manliness.[38] It would also make sense that the experiment – involving pure devotion and servitude – was one that saw itself above common carnal desire. Cullwick once said that she did not want children because of the pain of childbirth, so this may have been another disincentive to sexual intercourse.[39] John Ruskin, another associate, had a famously unconsummated marriage, possibly prompted by a desire to avoid children.[40]

But Cullwick and Munby certainly kissed and indulged in what they described as petting, 'her daily morning "petting"', as Munby termed it in 1893.[41] In 1870, Cullwick referred to 'the old sweet taste' of his lips refreshing her and reminding her how much she loved him.[42] There are descriptions of Cullwick kissing her husband 'fervently', clasping him round the waist and lifting him off the ground.[43] She told him that she had first kissed him because she wanted to see what his mouth was like. "'And what was it like?" "Oho! *nice*!" cried she ... "I know'd you was good, by the feel o' your mouth. An' I couldna love no man, if I didna like his mouth.'"[44] She also licked his face in the mornings ('and says that it is good for his eyes'); 'she is apt to use her tongue ... as a touch of affection'.[45] He wrote of the sweetness of her lips, 'her country lips which have the velvet touch'.[46] We also have Munby's report of their mutual bathing: she soaping him all over and rubbing him down in the morning, and he doing the same in the evening, in the same water, after she had spat in it to prevent their quarrelling (a Shropshire superstition):

To me it is nothing carnal or voluptuous, but a thing of infinite sacredness, the sight of her fair pure body: still plump and firm and strong, the healthy skin soft and pink-white everywhere, except on her face and neck and her robust round arms and roughened hands. And even all these were softened and made more delicate by the bath. I saw her safe into bed, and came down again to write.

The lines of gender and class are plain. She bathes in his dirty water, not vice versa. Cullwick is his wife and slave when she washes him: his reciprocation is almost a sacred act. Her body is not a sexual object to him, Munby stresses; the wife goes upstairs to bed alone. But the very recognition of the potentially 'voluptuous' and 'carnal' is surely significant, and it would be extremely difficult to desexualize their interaction. The text is most sexual when trying to erase its sexuality.[47]

Nor do they seem to have been inordinately reticent in their conversation. Cullwick did not blush (the textual blush) when telling her husband of the birth trauma of a neighbour – 'doctor says as her passage inna big enough for a two shillin piece!'[48] – or when she remembered the departure of the Shropshire pitwomen to seasonal labour in the market gardens near London, their men kissing the wheels of the coach and calling out to them to keep their legs closed until they got back.[49] On one occasion, when she read to Munby from the Bible at breakfast time and came to the story of the hundred foreskins of the Philistines, she said 'with a sly smile, "Eh, Massa! wouldn't that be a pretty dish!"'[50]

There was also a sexual component in the games that they played. On at least one occasion, Cullwick pretended to be Munby's landlady, 'speaking with the mincing manner of a lodginghouse keeper', playing to the full the sexual innuendo associated with the world of lodgers, and with Munby responding in kind: '"I have no objection to a reasonable charge for any of your attentions", ... and so the little comedy goes on for a while.' '"Oh Sir", she said, "if any one knowed as you had kissed me behind this door, my repitation in the parish 'ud be gone for ever!"'[51]

Before they married, she slept with a flannel shirt of his, draping the sleeve around her neck.[52] The powerful yet controlled sexuality is revealed in an incident which happened in the early period of their courtship, when Munby visited Cullwick while her employers were out of the house. He managed to persuade her to take off her servant's dress and try on her mistress's black and crimson ball gown. She 'hesitated to profane the Missis's things by touching them, much more, by wearing them; but to please me, she consented'. Although it would not fit properly (her waist was too big), she managed to squeeze into the dress; Munby brushed out her hair, 'in lady's fashion', and placed a rose in it. He was amazed by the transformation: 'I gazed on her in a kind of rapture: so lovely a figure she was, so lady like, so sweet, that I longed "to take her away from her slaving", and make of her a lady indeed.' He asked her to turn around and look in a large mirror.

The effect of this revelation was startling ... for the first time she noticed that her neck and bosom, and even her shoulders, were bare. Dazzling white, they seemed, by contrast with her hardworking arms ... in an instant they were suffused, like her face, with one universal blush – celestial rosyred, love's proper hue. She shut her eyes, turned sharply from the glass, and suddenly flung herself into my arms – 'that I might rather feel than see the beating of her heart'. 'Oh, Massa, she whispered, 'I am naked!' Never before had I felt so strongly the need for self control in her presence: never, before or since, have I been filled with a more passionate ardour of love and reverence for that pure and innocent soul ['rustic' is crossed out], who had trusted herself so utterly to me.[53]

The whole description, written decades after it occurred, is suffused with sexuality: the intrusion into a stranger's bedroom and thrill of the profanation of the mistress' clothing by the servant; undressing; the shock of class-defined 'nakedness'; blushing white flesh; the power of self-control. (One is reminded of the sexualization of innocence in Gothic fiction: 'the inexpressible charm of Modesty'.)[54] Literary critics have located different discourses of female sexuality in nineteenth-century England, represented by the threateningly sexual and by controlled (though not sexless) purity. The women in George Eliot's novels *Adam Bede* and *The Mill on the Floss*, Margaret Homans has argued, signify these sexualities in what she has termed 'Dinah's blush' and 'Maggie's arm', with the blush signifying erotic purity, and the arm a sign of expansive (working-class) sexuality.[55] In Cullwick, Munby had both the blush and the arms.

IV

It is significant that we should have concluded a previous section with a reference to opera. Performance was central to Munby's sexuality. Consider this brief description of Cullwick's rival, Sarah Carter, a farmer's daughter. Like Hannah, she was of hidden gentility, though in Carter's case she was actually 'ladyborn' and had fallen economically. And, like Hannah, she transported Munby 'to the very limit of selfcontrol'. Sarah Carter even cleaned his boots for him, conscious of the pleasure 'of a complex & doubtful kind' that it gave him. Though resonant of the fetishized rituals of Hannah, this performance was even more socially deadly:

No, I cannot talk now: here she stands – she who sings Mendelssohn with me to her own piano, who has all the feelings & much of the culture of a lady, & who *is* a lady by rights – here she stands, with her sweet face & sunny curls, cleaning boots in an outhouse; cleaning *my* boots.[56]

(This passage does not appear in Hudson's biography.) It should be clear by now that Munby's voyeurism was interactive, multi-layered and performative rather than mere detached gazing. The psychologist Alfred Binet, who first used the term 'sexual fetishism' in 1887, once referred to the 'love of the pervert' as a 'theater piece where a simple bit player advances to centre stage and takes the leading role'.[57] As a late twentieth-century German practitioner of masochism has put it, in the game of dominance and submission 'the entire spectrum of popular culture and a wide body of historical sources serve as scripts.'[58]

Zygmunt Bauman has described the *flâneur* as a kind of travelling player: 'To *flaner*, means to play the game of playing; a meta play of sorts. This play is conscious of itself as play. Its enjoyment is mature and pure. Or one may say: the job of the *flaneur* is to rehearse the world as theatre, life as a play.'

I see that man there meeting that woman. They stop, they talk. I do not know from where they came; I do not know what they are talking about; I do not know where they will go when they finish talking. Because I do not know all that and much more, I may make them into whatever I wish, all the more so that whatever I make them into will have no effect on what they are or will become. I am in charge; I invest their encounter with meaning; I may make him into a philanderer, her into a wife seeking escape from the grinding monotony of marriage; I may send them to bed right from where they stand at the moment, or to their respective rooms where they will sulk the missed chance. The power of my fantasy is the only limit the reality I imagine has, and the only it needs. To *flaner*, is to rehearse contingency of meaning; life as bagful of episodes none of which is definite, unequivocal, irreversible; life as a play.[59]

There are certainly elements of Munby in this description: life was fantasy, a play, a series of elaborate stages and scriptings, based on misconceived notions of hidden femininity and noble bloodlines. We may recall Cullwick's observation that their lives were like a play, 'only better [than] all the plays that ever was wrote'.[60] This book has staged the stagings: in city streets and village lanes; in cottage, drawing room, kitchen and dining room; at the pit mouth, blast furnace and cliff-face; in parks and gardens as well as fields; at the opera, exhibitions, galleries, the circus and music hall; on London Bridge and at the Derby; in the photographer's booth; and from courtroom to surgeon's consulting chamber. Munby's scripts included poetry, photography, painting, drawing, literature, drama, letters, diaries and novels, as he and the women involved in his fantasies read, wrote and played their lives. Their dramaturgy involved elaborate layers of playing, voyeurism and masquerade – passing, cleaning, watching, conversation, recording, secrecy. We have explored the dramatic scripting of these lives: the misalliance, the secret marriage, the peasant wife visited as an exhibit; the collected noseless ones – living corpses; the macabre stripping of femininity; the boot-licking and washing of feet and bodies; the demonstrations of female strength; the physiognomical way of seeing things; and the freighted handshake. We have negotiated the dramatic tropes: cleanliness/dirt, disfigurement/beauty, masculinity/femininity, slavery/mastery and animality/humanity. Yet we have detected little of the indeterminacy Bauman associates with *flânerie*. Munby's fantasies were carefully scripted; he knew their outcomes. Even his contingencies were rehearsed.

The term *fetishism* (in the sense of sexual fetishism) dates from the late nineteenth century, is normally associated with continental Europe and comes from the application of psychological notions of sexuality to an anthropological understanding of the term with respect to the worship of inanimate objects.[61] Binet captured the linkages perfectly:

These patients' adoration of inert objects such as night bonnets or boot nails resembles in all ways the adoration of the savage or the negro for fish bones or shiny stones, with the fundamental difference that, in our patient's cult, religious adoration is replaced by a sexual appetite.[62]

The essence of fetishism is overvaluation. The objects of this overvaluation could be a part of the body, clothing or a particular type of behaviour (including scopophilia: the pleasure of looking). The most common parts of the body likely to be fetishized, a modern account tells us, are the hand, foot, hair and eye; the most likely fetish-objects include boots, shoes, gloves and underwear (and materials such as fur, rubber and leather). As the Surrealists discovered, the power of fetishism lay in the conjunction of materiality (the touchable substance) and the psychological fantasy attached to that object: the 'imaginative leap'.[63] It was a leap that Munby experienced on an almost daily basis.

It has become conventional to attribute fetishism to early child-hood experiences. And the role of the nursemaid or servant looms large in such scenarios. A procession of cultural commentators have argued that servants mediated between the worlds of high and low, the lower-class street and the bourgeois home – a 'proletarian Trojan horse' is Alain Corbin's unforgettable description.[64] Such women traversed dirt and cleanliness. They disciplined the child, comforted him and were in a position to become the subject of his (the accounts are always in terms of the male) first conscious sexual experiences: the first-remembered sexual encounters of Walter and 'X' were with servants: '… servitude, erotic submission, and foot fetishism are curi-ously enmeshed within a complex system of representation centring on the maid.'[65] A woman on all fours, Peter Stallybrass and Allon White have written, was 'no exceptional scene in the nineteenth or early twentieth centuries'.[66] Such a contradictory mix at a formative age was powerfully constitutive of the types of desires exhibited by Munby (illus. 87–9).

Ann McClintock has listed the sadomasochistic elements in the Munby–Cullwick relationship:

Cullwick and Munby filled their lives with the theatrical paraphernalia of S/M: boots, chains, padlocks, leather, blindfolds, straps, costumes, scripts and photographs – some of them semi-pornographic. Their games included a variety of fetish rituals: transvestism, bondage, foot and leather fetishism, washing rituals, infantilism, animalism and voyeurism.[67]

Although her modernization of their interactions wrenches them out of context, McClintock's descriptions are a useful reminder of the sheer extent of Munby and Hannah's repertoire. We examined the complex and highly scripted rounds of dominance and submission in a previous chapter. We have also encountered a multiplicity of animate and inanimate fetishes employed by Munby: hands, skin (living and dead), noses (absent, present, false and real), masks and veils, arms and legs, trousers, boots, dirt, blackness, and lock and chain. The man who

87–9 A 'proletarian Trojan horse':
Hannah Cullwick, servant.

imagined his wife as a shoe was an innocent in comparison to the subject of this book. Munby was an archetypal fetishist.

V

The intriguing question about Munby's sexuality is the role of continence or celibacy amidst the fetishism. The motivations behind Victorian male continence were contradictory and varied. One obvious influence was 'anti-sensualism', a strong grain of personal control found in religious circles and also at a lower level among those keen to establish themselves as the more respectable sectors of the working class, a culture that stressed sexual restraint and morality.[68] The historical demographer Simon Szreter has linked anti-sensualism to the nineteenth-century fertility transition to small family size, arguing that marital continence (regulation and avoidance of sex in marriage) was an important means of contraception. Victorian couples employed contraception by avoidance of sex; they delayed marriage; they spaced births by sexual self-restraint, reducing the number of times that they had intercourse – practising what Szreter has called a 'culture of abstinence'.[69]

Another, somewhat different possibility is what has been termed cerebral lechery. As Wendy Graham has observed of the sexuality of the writer Henry James, it is important not to focus on genital sex as a proxy for sexual identity. James's sexuality privileged 'forepleasure', belonging more in the realm of the mind than the genitals.[70] He practised 'cerebral lechery ... by no means incompatible with total sexual abstinence'.[71] Graham quotes a contemporary, J. A. Symonds, to good effect:

Many a man who never stooped to any carnal deed has wallowed in the grossest sensuality of thought. Inside the sphere of their desires such men are agent and patient, double-sexed, immersed in epicene voluptuousness, for ever longing, for ever picturing delights, for ever unassuaged.[72]

One strand of cerebral lechery appealed to the jaded and the disillusioned, at one with the ennui expressed so often in the literature of *fin-de-siècle* Europe: 'No sexual pleasure offered by reality could possibly satisfy the desire of such a *debauche*. And so, the ideal of sexual gratification rises high above reality.'[73]

Munby, for all his cerebral sexuality, was hardly a *débauche*. His cerebralism was the only sexuality that he had ever known, and certainly not a product of ennui. Indeed, his cerebralism is all the more interesting for its link with male continence rather than debauchery. And yet while the culture of abstinence may describe the physical import of Munby's sexuality, it scarcely captures its psychology. What Arthur Munby seemed most attracted by – the greatest charge of all – was *resisting temptation*. McClintock has referred tellingly to his 'compulsive and perpetually deferred pleasures'.[74] Victorians recognized 'the power of desire and the danger of pleasure', Steven Seidman has argued, and much of their sexual history is a working out of ways of negotiating these tensions.[75] It was as if Munby eroticized the very containment of desire that

Seidman has found to be at the heart of Victorian middle-class sexual culture.

Celibate bachelorhood – even celibate marriage – was not unknown in the Victorian period; we have already referred to Ruskin's relationship. The writers J. M. Barrie and Henry James were both involved in long periods of (for want of a more accurate term) uncon-summated heterosexuality. For James – like Munby – it was a case of lifelong celibacy. Recent literary criticism has focused on the role of the celibate bachelor in Victorian texts, queering both the characters and their creators. Eve Kosofsky Sedgwick reads their 'sexual anaes-thesia' in the context of the history of homosexuality, a precursor to the more clearly forged identities of the late century. These bachelors were men with little genital contact with women but who were not involved in more obviously homosexual activity either. They were part of what she has termed male homosexual panic.[76] As already mentioned, two of the creators of these characters – Barrie and James – likewise experienced sexual anaesthesia. In this period before the construction of the more rigid binary of heterosexual and homosex-ual, such men can be interpreted as part of a sexual regime permitting more flexible and varied sexual identities.[77] Wendy Graham has argued that James's lack of genital activity made possible his homo-sexuality, expressed in the erotics of his letter-writing, his cerebral lechery.[78]

This book has not engaged in a thoroughgoing queering of Arthur Munby. As suggested in the previous chapter, it is possible that his focus on masculinized women's bodies was a code for deeper desires; or that his feelings of powerlessness in the face of female masculinity – his feminization – indicated same-sex tendencies. It might be possi-ble to move towards a more sophisticated reading along the lines of the work on Henry James. Such a project could further explore the way in which male bodies were invoked in contrast to the strength and power of Munby's hybrid women. Or it could analyze Munby as bachelor, for he spent most of his life in the company of men, and his strong male friendships and homosocial interactions are indisputable. Recall that his marriage to Cullwick was clandestine: Munby was a bachelor to most of those who knew him.[79] Surely, it is also significant that he moved on the fringes of the Pre-Raphaelite Brotherhood, whose homo-erotic bondings have recently been proposed by Herbert Sussman.[80]

While not wanting to foreclose queer readings, I have privileged Munby's fascination with the absent feminine rather than the absent masculine. His obsession – as I am sure readers will have grasped –

was woman. His homosexuality, if it existed, was very heavily coded indeed. But perhaps that is the whole point. Attempts to press him into the hetero/homo binary are simply inappropriate in the Victorian context of multiple sexualities. Munby demonstrates the slipperiness of sexual categories. His story displays the complexity of Victorian sexual identities, what has been described as the 'remarkable variousness of Victorian sexuality'.[81]

In this context, it is worth pausing for a moment to consider the case of George Moore, the celebrated Irish-born London novelist, friend of Zola, Manet and Degas, and author of, among many works, mostly long forgotten, *Esther Waters* (1894), the story of a fallen maidservant. Moore was fascinated by the rejection of marriage and sexual procreation, writing a series of novellas on the theme of what his most recent biographer, Adrian Frazier, has aptly termed 'the secret workings of sex in those who don't have sex'.[82] Mildred Lawson, one of the characters in *Celibates* (1895), flirted but remained chaste: 'She knew that her safety lay in her chastity' (although a rival wondered whether her thoughts were 'equally chaste': an accusation of cerebral lechery perhaps?).[83] Another character in one of Moore's early novels is repelled by the thought of sexual relations with a woman (one of the charges laid against John Ruskin's unconsummated marriage)[84] and decides on a life of secular celibacy, with the 'world' as his 'monastery'.[85] John Norton, who appears again in *Celibates*, is a man who has conquered his temptations; a *flâneur* who enjoys the 'spectacle of life': 'I am an onlooker.' Norton claims at one point that he is

not suited to married life. There is a better and purer life to lead ... an inner life, coloured and permeated with feelings and tones that are intensely our own. He who may live this life shrinks from any adventitious presence that might jar it.

Chastity brought him 'peace of mind'[86]:

Recollection of Plato floated upon his weak brain, and he remembered that the great philosopher had said that there were men who were half women, and that these men must perforce delight in the society of women. That there were men too who were wholly men, and that these perforce could find neither pleasure nor interest away from their own sex. He had always felt himself to be wholly male, and this was why the present age, so essentially the age of women, was repellent to him.

Kitty, the one woman who does not provoke feelings of repulsion in Norton, is described as 'sexless as a work of art': 'She seemed to him purged, as a Greek statue, of all life's grossness.' Significantly, she has 'reedy, translucid hands'.[87]

Moore's later collection, *Celibate Lives*, contains a tale of giddy sexual possibilities about a woman – the appropriately named *and large-nosed* Albert Nobbs – who masquerades as a male servant until s/he is discovered by another young man, who is also really a woman. It is a story of 'perhapsers', of beings 'neither man nor woman': of one woman in men's clothes married to one in petticoats; of another contemplating marriage to a love-abandoned servant girl, raising her illegitimate child as 'his' own; and of fantasies of the two, or three, (wo)men setting up house together.[88]

Moore is more easily queered than Munby, and Frazier has traced his somewhat tantalizing relationships with homosexuals and homosexuality.[89] He was subject to (still unresolved) rumours about sexual impotence, was horrified at the prospect of generating life, never married and enjoyed strong male friendships: for six years, he lived, like Munby, at the Temple, a centre of London literary homosociality. And yet, as with Munby, it is the difficulty of sexual categorization that is so notable. Both men have been described as voyeurs of young women, though Moore was certainly more (hetero)sexually active than the protagonist of our story. (Frazier refers to Moore's facility with his tongue in love as well as literature.)[90] Both men collected young women. Moore's method was through literary co-endeavour, and his work, in its various forms, including his letter-writing ('sex through the transatlantic post'), was a means of intensifying desire: a letter to one of his female friends refers to a sexual feeling beyond 'its simplest form'.[91] Frazier observes that his subject is

happiest when sex is polymorphous: that is, when it is transferred from genital intercourse to touch and talk, to sight and speculation, to future prospects or long retrospection, where it can be indefinitely prolonged through thought. Sex that is only speculative, or better yet, speculations that are sexualised, he preferred to the brief deed of procreation.[92]

Similar observations could be made of Munby's 'sociology'.

Perhaps parasexuality comes closest to engaging with Munby's (and Moore's) world. *Parasexuality* is Peter Bailey's useful term for a type of Victorian sexuality, quite open in its expression, flirtatious, but stopping short of more serious sexual involvement. Parasexuality is sex 'deployed but contained': 'everything but'.[93] Bailey has advanced the barmaid as the central character – the object of desire – in parasexuality, but it could be just as likely have been a music-hall entertainer (male or female), an acrobat, actor or actress, or, as we have seen in this book, any number of performers from opera to minstrelsy. Parasexuality, then, could be applied beyond the bar to dance halls, theatre, parks, races and streets – anywhere where the sexes gathered and interacted without necessarily progressing to more serious sex. It is particularly interesting as a phenomenon because it hovers somewhere in the middle of theories of repression or permissiveness. Parasexuality represents a certain amount of freedom of interaction, but with simultaneous control.

Yet parasexuality does not sufficiently describe the multiple layers of Munby's longing, and the desires of those who were involved with him. Hence I have resorted to inventing my own term, *permasexuality*, to capture the sheer sexualization of Munby's interactions and ways of seeing. By this, I do not mean to invoke the 'perma' of permafrost, meaning a permanent upper level, though I do not quarrel with its implications for the longevity and intensity of the sexualities that I have been outlining. I have in mind more the permeational aspect of 'perma'. I want to convey a sexualization that permeated life and culture, representations and perceptions. In more recent parlance, 'perm' is also short for 'permute', meaning a variety of possible combinations or arrangements.[94] This sense of the word also conveys the type of sexuality revealed by our case study, sexuality that involved both continence and longing: sex as truly polymorphous.[95]

Postscript

Arthur Munby's volume of poems *Relicta* (1909) contains a bizarre, dream-like poem about an ape-woman. The narrator encounters an ape chained in a tree – a fierce, strong, hairy creature. But there is something in the animal's eyes that leads him to believe that she (the ape's sex is established from the outset) is actually a woman. Later, in the dining room of the hotel in which he is staying, he sees a woman in the corner and recognizes her gaze:

> Sure, I remember those bright brown eyes?
> And the self-same look that in them lies
> I have seen already, with strange surprise,
> This very afternoon;
> Not in the face of a woman like this,
> Who has human features, and lips to kiss.
> But in one who can only splutter and hiss –
> In the eyes of a grim baboon!

The beast has to be restrained from attacking the poet. The voyeur's gaze is returned. The ape/woman 'grinn'd and sputter'd and gazed at me', writes the poet; 'She did not like my scrutiny.' It is the first time that the voyeur displays any hint of insecurity regarding the power of his gaze.[1]

Munby's poem was based on a meeting with Julia Pastrana, a human exhibit famous throughout Europe and North America in the 1850s. Paraded as the 'Marvellous Hybrid' in halls and rooms from Baltimore to Warsaw, the subject of a learned paper in the *Lancet* and mentioned in Darwin's *Variation of Animals and Plants*, Pastrana was exhibited before a variety of medical and anthropological experts as well as performing on the stage and at fairs and circuses. It would be unwise to separate the scientific from baser entertainment, however: the naturalist Frank Buckland was captivated by the contrast between Pastrana's hideous hairiness and her 'good and graceful' figure and 'tiny foot and well-turned ankle, *bien chaussé*, perfection itself'.[2]

Munby first saw her in 1857:

Litchfield and I went to see a creature whose hideous portrait was placarded all over London, as 'Julia Pastrana, The Nondescript'. A being in woman's clothes, and with hands & feet not only human but very shapely; but of bestial aspect – her dark olive skin covered thinly with black hair, over nearly the whole body: her face the face of an ape, hairy all over – having enormous lips, an abnormal tongue, faunlike tufted ears, and a peaked faunlike beard; a profusion however of coarse black woman's hair on the head. The eyes, as I remember, had nothing human in their appearance or expression. She smoked vehemently: I gave her a cigarette, which she eagerly seized, and seating herself in an apish posture astride of a tall chair, she lighted it and smoked it through; looking a perfect fiend, as she sat there before the spectators, her great cavernous eyes flaming and her huge nostrils omitting clouds of smoke. Yet with all this, she was substantially human: she spoke several languages, sang, danced, was lively and intelligent. Of her origin nothing certain was or is known: the story however being that her mother was a Mexican Indian, who was lost for years in a country full of apes & bears.

It is held, I believe, that such an union as is thus hinted at can never produce conception; the spermatozoa of beasts being unable to germinate in the human female, and vice versa? Moreover a detailed inspection of this creature was all in favour of her humanity, in spite of her fearfully bestial appearance & her brutish ways: but still, if ever there was a suspicious case it was this; and the tremendous issues of the problem gave a hideous fascination to the case.[3]

Pastrana left London with her husband and manager, Theodore Lent, to lucrative tours through Berlin, Leipzig, Vienna, Warsaw and Moscow. She died in Russia in 1860, shortly after giving birth to a baby boy who also died. But her days as an exhibited freak were by no means over, for the bodies were embalmed by a Russian taxidermist, and mother and child returned to London for display, first to a select few as medical curiosities, and then to the public for a shilling admission.[4] (The pair were exhibited in fairgrounds in the US and Scandinavia as late as the 1970s.) Munby saw the dead Pastrama again in Piccadilly in 1862, in a room at the Burlington Gallery:

... there, on a pedestal in the middle of the floor, stood 'The embalmed Nondescript', as they call her now, looking exactly as in life. Wearing a short ballet-dress, which I was told she made for herself; her legs cased in pink stockings, her feet planted wide apart, just as she used to stand – like an animal painfully reared on its hindlegs; her coarse black hair wreathed with flowers; bracelets on the bare and hirsute arms; and a *wedding ring* upon the hard dead hand![5]

The themes and imagery of the poem and diary entries will have some resonances for readers of this book. The poet experiences fascinated horror: 'a thrill of shuddering awe', which 'thrill'd me through and through' (see Chapter 2). There are familiar feelings of helplessness and impotence in the face of female strength (see Chapters 3 and 5):

> Perhaps she would get at me, after all!
> If the links should break, I might well feel small,
> Young as I was, and strong and tall,
> And blest with a human shape,
> To see myself foil'd in that lonely place
> By a desperate brute with a monstrous face,
> And hugg'd to death in the foul embrace
> Of a loathly angry ape.[6]

The 'ape' hangs like a 'human acrobat' and, in her preserved (and touchable) state, wears the short dress and pink stockings of a dancer or high-wire performer (see Chapter 4). The fetishist is even provided with a dead hand with a wedding ring.

Most palpable are the repeated slippages between woman and animal. With its underlying hint of bestiality, the literal merging of human and animal, and its multiple hybridities of masculinity and femininity, ape and woman, and, after her embalming, life and death, Julia Pastrana's body provides a heightened return to the horrors played out around the noseless women and the disordering bodies of Munby's working-class subjects, especially the grotesque caricatures of the pitwomen (illus. 90). The fragility of the barrier between human and animal, and the fascination with the possibility of the existence of living 'missing links', were proclaimed, literally, in the exhibiting of the 'Nondescript'. Like an exaggerated version of Degas' wax, hair and fabric sculpture *Little Dancer Aged Fourteen* (illus. 91), whose model critics condemned as 'among the most odiously ugly ... the standard of horror and bestiality', Pastrana's body was a visual expression of male fears of the feminine at the *fin de siècle*[7]:

As results of embalming, they are wonderful; but the hideous hairy face of this dead Julia Pastrana, staring at you with great glass eyes, & crowned with a ghastly contrast of gay flowers, is enough to fill your fancy with nightmares. It is like seeing a stuffed ape in woman's clothes, & knowing that it is a woman after all.[8]

Munby returned later to buy a photograph of her.[9]

As we have seen, the stories surrounding Munby involve multiple cultural histories: horror, fetishism, voyeurism, fears of degeneration, and Victorian sexuality. But all the stories we have heard return to one theme: woman. And his obsession with ideals of femininity and their

90 Femininity dislocated: a pitwoman.

dislocations ends fittingly with this slippage from woman to animal in the ape-woman. There is manifest irony in the meaning of Munby's representations, for the Preface to his poem *Dorothy* contains a critique of generations of polite literary and artistic endeavour which had erased the reality of working feminine bodies – 'black faces and hard hands'. Where are the large hands in the beautiful heroines of Fielding, Richardson and Scott? Even Shakespeare was oblivious to the 'pathetic contrast between a sweet young face and a pair of work-worn hands'.[10] The clue to my argument lies with that phrase 'pathetic contrast'. The very appeal of Munby's bodily de-formations was the reinforcement of the 'other''s other, the feminine ideal (illus. 92). Through disrupting this ideal with notions of largeness, blackness, strength, coarseness and deformity, the psychological effect was actually to increase the power of the absent image. The force of Munby's imagery lay with its reinforcement of the very stereotypes of femininity he claimed to be rejecting.

There is a tendency to see Munby as a man of two worlds (the

91 Fears of the feminine: This figure's supposed simian physiognomy indicated her criminal/lower-class origins, degeneracy, and flowering depravity (Edgar Degas, *Little Dancer Aged Fourteen*, plaster version, 1880–81).

92 Woman's masculine/feminine mirror: the 'other''s other.

subtitle of his biography): the realm of poets, artists and writers, and the domain of hands and working women. However, Munby's worlds were not separate; they were inseparable. There is a marvellous description of their integration in his own narration of an evening at the Chelsea home of Dante Gabriel Rossetti. The small group examined Rossetti's sketches of Browning and Swinburne and his idealized portraits of William Morris's beautiful wife, Jane Burden, with her 'glorious heroic face'. (The woman whose body, Herbert Sussman has commented, was the occasion for the homoerotic attraction between Rossetti and Morris.) While they talked, Rossetti nursed his Canadian marmot. They then went upstairs to dine on a white table filled with antique china, glass and silver, and to discuss 'literature, poetry, art'. The dinner, 'elaborate and refined', was served by a female servant, 'a robust and comely young matron, whose large strong hands, used to serving, contrast with the small hands of her master, used to pictures and to poems' (the hands which had been stroking the marmot, minutes before).[11]

While we have been exploring one man's fantasies, the intention is not to parade Munby as a freak. His obsessions were not unique. As several historians have noted, there was a strong strand of sexual voyeurism in the surveys of the Victorian social investigators.[12] And Charles Dickens, who made particular use of 'hands' as a device in his literature, was also a *flâneur*.[13] We have already referred to the Ovidian myth of Pygmalion and Galatea as a European cultural commonplace, a recurring trope – from the Enlightenment philosophical couple of eighteenth-century France who reject marriage for 'a looser kind of alliance, based on mutual interest and affection', to 'Pygmalionism', the sexologists' taxonomy for a perverted sexual interest in statues, 'a rare form of erotomania'.[14] The myth of Pygmalion can be found in ballet, music, novels, opera, painting, poetry, sculpture and theatre; in Rousseau, Goethe, Voltaire, Bach, Herder, Hazlitt, Beddoes, Coleridge, Browning, W. S. Gilbert, Rodin and Frederick Tennyson.[15]

Hence Munby's significance lies in his cultural context, for although his blend of desires was truly peculiar, he was very much a man of his time. After all, Gustave Flaubert, Sigmund Freud and Walter Benjamin are all invoked to describe the importance of the maid in nineteenth- and early twentieth-century male bourgeois sexuality.[16] Scopophilia, the sexual pleasure of looking, was scarcely confined to Munby; Abigail Solomon-Godeau has referred to the erotic spectacle of the nineteenth-century ballet, the 'bazaar of legs', focus of the 'fetishizing gaze of the male spectator'.[17] Edgar Degas exhibited a comparable combination of voyeurism, sexual anaesthesia

93 The parasexual Folies: Edouard Manet, *A Bar at the Folies Bergère*, 1881–2.

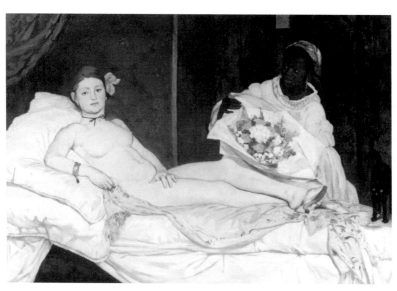

94 'A coal lady from Batignolles'/'Apes on a bed' (Edouard Manet, *Olympia*, 1863–5).

95 Caricature of Manet's *Olympia*, showing how the painting was viewed; note the large, dirty hands and feet ('Promenades au Salon, par cham', *Le Charivari*, 1865).

and fascination with working women (in his case, café singers, dancers and laundresses).[18] George Moore once wrote that the art of Degas had created a *nouveau frisson*: 'The short, coarse, thick thighs of the poor working woman, deformed by the toil of modern days, have never been seen on canvas before.'[19] Thus Griselda Pollock has warned against the fetishizing of Munby, arguing that several key nineteenth-century writers and artists shared his 'fascination with the complex of dirt, bodies, sex and female labour'.[20] When Pollock reviewed Edouard Manet's canonical *A Bar at the Folies Bergère* (illus. 93), she fastened on the bare hands of the barmaid and the boots and legs of the trapeze artist in the top left-hand corner of the picture, explaining their erotic significance for nineteenth-century bourgeois male viewers.[21] With its blend of 'exoticism, danger, and sexuality' the parasexual Folies were a 'flaneur's paradise'.[22] Nor was there anything singular about Munby's delight in the disruption of the bodily conventions of masculinity and femininity; Tamar Garb has demonstrated comparable tendencies in the art of Gustave Caillebotte and Paul Cézanne.[23]

This book started with a well-known image, so it is fitting that we conclude with another: Manet's famous painting *Olympia*, the subject of much spilling of critical ink. One of the main issues has been why there was such an over-reaction to this painting of a reclining, naked woman, her black servant and a cat (illus. 94). I want to finish by suggesting that Munby's shared obsessions hold a vital key, for the critics focused on Olympia's body in ways that should be familiar to readers of this book. Olympia was a 'coal lady from Batignolles'. The cartoons caricaturing the painting stressed the non-human nature of her body: they inscribe large and dirty hands and feet (illus. 95). Descriptions slip into animality. *Le Grand Journal* deemed her 'a sort of female gorilla ... apes on a bed'. Moreover, her image was corpse-like: dirty, deformed, recalling 'the horror of the morgue' with the 'livid tint of a cadaver displayed in the morgue'. Olympia lay there 'like a corpse on the counters at the morgue'.[24] In this one response to a famous cultural icon of the nineteenth century, we get a mirror-image of Munby's slippages from woman to beast to death. And there is a sexual subtext: Olympia was a prostitute.[25]

References

Preface

1 Charles Baudelaire, 'The Painter of Modern Life', in *Baudelaire: Selected Writings on Art and Artists*, trans. P. E. Charvet (Cambridge, 1981), pp. 399–400.

2 The diaries and letters of Arthur J. Munby (1828–1910) and Hannah Cullwick (1833–1909), Trinity College Library, Cambridge [hereafter referred to as Munby], vol. 64, pp. 81–2.

3 D. Hudson, *Munby, Man of Two Worlds: The Life and Diaries of Arthur J. Munby 1828–1910* [1972] (London, 1974); L. Davidoff, 'Class and Gender in Victorian England', *Feminist Studies*, 5 (1979), reprint in J. L. Newton, M. P. Ryan and J. R. Walkowitz, eds, *Sex and Class in Women's History* (London, 1983), chap. 1.

4 Munby 12, pp. 162–3.

5 Davidoff, 'Class and Gender'; M. Hiley, *Victorian Working Women: Portraits from Life* (London, 1979); A. V. John, *By the Sweat of Their Brow: Women Workers at Victorian Coal Mines* (London, 1980); L. Stanley, ed., *The Diaries of Hannah Cullwick, Victorian Maidservant* (London, 1984); P. Stallybrass and A. White, *The Politics and Poetics of Transgression* (Ithaca, 1986), chap. 4; L. Stanley, 'Biography as Microscope or Kaleidoscope? The Case of Hannah Cullwick's Relationship with Arthur Munby', *Studies in Sexual Politics*, 13/14 (1986), pp. 28–46; H. Dawkins, 'The Diaries and Photographs of Hannah Cullwick', *Art History*, 10 (1987), pp. 154–87; J. Swindells, 'Liberating the Subject? Autobiography and "Women's History": A Reading of *The Diaries of Hannah Cullwick*', in J. W. Barbre and others, eds, *Interpreting Women's Lives* (Bloomington, 1989), pp. 24–38; G. Pollock, 'The Dangers of Proximity: The Spaces of Sexuality and Surveillance in Word and Image', *Discourse*, 16 (1993–4), pp. 3–50; G. Pollock, '"With My Own Eyes": Fetishism, the Labouring Body and the Colour of Its Sex', *Art History*, 17 (1994), pp. 342–82; C. Mavor, *Pleasures Taken: Performances of Sexuality and Loss in Victorian Photographs* (Durham, NC, 1995), chap. 3; A. McClintock, *Imperial Leather: Race, Gender and Sexuality in the Colonial Context* (London, 1995), chaps 2–3; M. MacLure, 'Eccentric Subject, Impossible Object: A Poststructural Reading of Hannah Cullwick', *Qualitative Studies in Education*, 10 (1997), pp. 315–32; R. Allen, 'Munby Reappraised: The Diary of an English Flaneur', *Journal of Victorian Culture*, 5 (2000), pp. 260–86. There is a disturbing lack of intertextuality in some of these studies. The work of Dawkins and (particularly) Pollock anticipates that of McClintock, although Pollock's presumably appeared too late to be included in *Imperial Leather*. MacLure and Allen seem unaware of several of the studies that preceded theirs; Allen refers to a 'recent near-silence' in studies of Munby (p. 261)!

6 B. Creed, *The Monstrous-feminine: Film, Feminism, Psychoanalysis* (London,

1993), p. 29.

7 I am referring to Laura Mulvey's much-reprinted essay, 'Visual Pleasure and Narrative Cinema' (1975); see her *Visual and Other Pleasures* (London, 1989), chap. 3. For a summary of theories of spectatorship and developments since Mulvey, see P. Erens, ed., *Issues in Feminist Film Criticism* (Bloomington and Indianapolis, 1990); J. Mayne, *The Woman at the Keyhole: Feminism and Women's Cinema* (Bloomington and Indianapolis, 1990), chap. 1; S. Hayward, *Key Concepts in Cinema Studies* (London, 1996), pp. 331–7.

8 L. Devereaux, 'An Introductory Essay', in L. Devereaux and R. Hillman, eds, *Fields of Vision: Essays in Film Studies, Visual Anthropology, and Photography* (Berkeley and Los Angeles, 1995), p. 10.

9 C. Gledhill, 'Pleasurable Negotiations', in E. D. Pribram, ed., *Female Spectators: Looking at Film and Television* (London, 1988), chap. 4.

10 See n. 5 above.

11 Mavor, *Pleasures Taken*, pp. 78, 84.

12 S. Marcus, *The Other Victorians: A Study of Sexuality and Pornography in Mid-nineteenth Century England* (London, 1966).

13 For a useful summary of the historiographical context, see F. Mort and L. Nead, 'Sexuality, Modernity and the Victorians', *Journal of Victorian Culture*, 1 (1996), pp. 118–30; S. Szreter, 'Victorian Britain, 1831–1963: Towards a Social History of Sexuality', *Journal of Victorian Culture*, 1 (1996), pp. 136–49.

14 Hudson, *Munby*, p. 4.

15 M. Foucault, *The History of Sexuality* [1976] (London, 1979).

16 *Ibid.*, p. 17.

17 J. Weeks, *Sex, Politics and Society: The Regulation of Sexuality since 1800* (London, 1989), esp. chap. 2. See also P. Anderson, *When Passion Reigned: Sex and the Victorians* (Oxford, 1995); A. H. Miller and J. E. Adams, 'Introduction', in *idem*, eds, *Sexualities in Victorian Britain* (Bloomington, 1996), pp. 1–15.

18 N. Annan, 'Under the Victorian Bed', *New York Review of Books*, 22 June 1995.

19 Hudson, *Munby*, pp. 10, 70.

20 P. Gay, *The Bourgeois Experience, Victoria to Freud*: vol. 1: *Education of the Senses* (Oxford, 1984); M. Mason, *The Making of Victorian Sexuality* (Oxford, 1994); *idem*, *The Making of Victorian Sexual Attitudes* (Oxford, 1994).

21 Liz Stanley has edited selections of Cullwick's diaries (see n. 5 above), but I have drawn on a wider range, including numerous unpublished letters from Cullwick to Munby. Historians have made little use of Munby's diaries describing his visits to Cullwick during the later stages of their relationship, so most of this material (used in Chapter 3) is new. Nor has there been any previous sustained attempt to deal with Munby's disfigured women (see Chapter 2).

1 Watching Hannah

1 J. Wolf, 'The Culture of Separate Spheres: The Role of Culture in Nineteenth-century Public and Private Life', in her *Feminine Sentences: Essays on Women and Culture* (Oxford, 1990), chap. 2. For an introduction to this complex and contentious historiography, see A. Vickery, 'Golden Age to Separate Spheres? A Review of the Categories and Chronology of English Women's History', *Historical Journal*, 36 (1993), pp. 383–414.

2 J. Ruskin, *Sesame and Lilies* (London, 1970), pp. 59–60. (Wolf, *Feminine Sentences*, p. 16, also quotes this passage.)

3 Ruskin, *Sesame and Lilies*, pp. 49–50, 58.

4 *Ibid.*, pp. 66–7.

5 *Ibid.*, pp. 60–63.

6 *Ibid.*, p. 60.

7 L. Nead, *Myths of Sexuality: Representations of Women in Victorian Britain* (Oxford, 1988), chap. 1.

8 The diaries and letters of Arthur J. Munby (1828–1910) and Hannah Cullwick (1833–1909), Trinity College Library, Cambridge [hereafter referred to as Munby], vol. 17, pp. 80–81.

9 D. Hudson, *Munby, Man of Two Worlds: The Life and Diaries of Arthur J. Munby 1828–1910* (London, 1974), p. 231.

10 Munby 82, pp. 216–20.

11 *Ibid.*; Munby 17, pp. 80–81.

12 Munby 14, p. 223.

13 Hudson, *Munby,* p. 3. For the historiography of Arthur Munby and Hannah Cullwick, see Preface, n. 5.

14 Munby 8, p. 207.

15 'The Living Stream at London Bridge', *London Society,* 3 (1863), p. 213.

16 Quoted in M. Cowling, *The Artist as Anthropologist: The Representation of Type and Character in Victorian Art* (Cambridge, 1989), p. 248.

17 Munby 19, pp. 108–13.

18 Munby 37, 26 June 1869.

19 Munby, 64, p. 51.

20 For London as Babylon (a nineteenth-century characterization), see L. Nead, *Victorian Babylon: People, Streets and Images in Nineteenth-century London* (London, 2000), p. 3.

21 Munby 26, pp. 42–6.

22 See T. C. Davis, *Actresses as Working Women: Their Social Identity in Victorian Culture* (London, 1991), chap. 5.

23 Munby 12, pp. 10–31.

24 *Ibid.*, pp. 176–81.

25 Most recently, R. Allen, 'Munby Reappraised: The Diary of an English Flaneur', *Journal of Victorian Culture,* 5 (2000), pp. 260–86.

26 Munby 41, 19 September 1873, recalling what he had seen in 1843.

27 Munby 97, Book 2, 22 September 1865.

28 Munby 37, 30 December 1869: for use of dialect.

29 Munby 6, pp. 35–6.

30 Munby 26, pp. 97–127; Munby 35, 21 September 1867.

31 Munby 6, p. 46.

32 Munby 8, pp. 220–21.

33 *Ibid.*, pp. 202–4.

34 Munby 6, pp. 30, 32, 34.

35 Munby 14, pp. 40–52.

36 *Ibid.*, pp. 192–203.

37 *Ibid.*, pp. 40–52.

38 'Passing Faces', *Household Words,* 14 April 1855.

39 'The Education of the Streets', *London Society,* 34 (1878), p. 483.

40 For Mayhew, C. Herbert, 'Mayhew's Cockney Polynesia', in his *Culture and Anomie: Ethnographic Imagination in the Nineteenth Century* (Chicago, 1991), chap. 4, is particularly helpful.

41 Munby 6, pp. 231–3.

42 Munby 14, pp. 141–5.

43 Munby 84, p. 170.

44 See her diaries: for example, Munby 98/4 (1870).

45 See Munby 98/2 (1864).

46 Munby 16, p. 247.

47 Munby 18, pp. 50–53.

48 Munby 98/2 (1864).

49 Munby 42, p. 7.

50 Munby 40, p. 111.

51 Munby 45, p. 5.

52 Munby 41, 10 June 1873.

53 Munby 42, p. 22.

54 *Ibid.*, pp. 36–7.

55 Munby 99/59 (2).

56 *Ibid.*

57 Munby 83, p. 181.

58 Munby's description of 'rustic Acton': Munby, 17, pp. 157–8.

59 Munby 41, 29 May 1873.

60 Munby 81, pp. ii–iii.

61 *Ibid.*, pp. 14–15.

62 *Ibid.*, p. 8.

63 *Ibid.*, p. 10.

64 Munby 82, p. 111.

65 *Ibid.*, pp. 115–16.

66 *Ibid.*, pp. 85–120.

67 Munby 91, pp. 78–9. Sketch facing p. 1.

68 Munby 63, p. 96.

69 Munby 81, pp. 41–3.

70 Munby 80, pp. 8–17 for the vicar's visit.

71 Munby 91, p. 174.

72 Munby 81, p. 72.

73 *Ibid.*, p. 110.

74 Munby 87, p. 99.

75 Munby 42, p. 17.

76 *Ibid.*, p. 46.

77 Munby 70, pp. 43a–47a.

78 Munby 87, p. 3.

79 Munby 108/83 (1): 'Hannah's Home'.

80 Munby 1, pp. 158–60.

2 Harriet's Nose: Horror, Bodily De-formation and Femininity

1 R. Barthes, *Camera Lucida* (London, 1993), esp. pp. 26–7.

2 See S. L. Gilman, 'The Phantom of the Opera's Nose', in his *Health and Illness: Images of Difference* (London, 1995), chap. 4.

3 E. Gerard [Emily de Laszowska], *The Tragedy of a Nose* (London, 1898). Hugo takes ultimate satisfaction in the fact that Wenzel's genes will not pass on the beautiful nose; the novella ends with a description of a tribe of young snub-nosed Wondraczeks.

4 N. Gogol, 'The Nose' [1836], in *Diary of a Madman and Other Stories* (Harmondsworth, 1972), pp. 42–70.

5 The diaries and letters of Arthur J. Munby (1828–1910) and Hannah Cullwick (1833–1909), Trinity College Library, Cambridge [hereafter referred to as Munby], vol. 1, pp. 12–14.

6 *Ibid*, p. 30.

7 Munby 4, pp. 59–62.

8 D. Hudson, *Munby, Man of Two Worlds: The Life and Diaries of Arthur J. Munby*

1828–1910 (London, 1974), p. 393.

9 Although Liz Stanley did briefly discuss the implications of this 'collection' for her view of Munby: L. Stanley, 'Biography as Microscope or Kaleidoscope? The Case of Hannah Culwick's Relationship with Arthur Munby', *Studies in Sexual Politics*, 13/14 (1986), esp. pp. 38–40.

10 See Munby 1, pp. 176–7; Munby 5, pp. 200–204, 229–30; Munby 8, pp. 129–30, 185–6; Munby 14, pp. 212–17, 240–41; Munby 29, 23 April 1861.

11 Munby 9, pp. 178–80.

12 *Ibid.*, pp. 209–12.

13 Munby 13, pp. 74–82.

14 *Ibid.*, pp. 256–7.

15 Munby 14, pp. 71–3.

16 *Ibid.*, pp. 82–4.

17 Munby 34, 16 October 1866.

18 *Ibid.*, 25 October 1866.

19 *Ibid.*, 6 November 1866.

20 Munby 14, p. 146.

21 Munby 33, 24 and 29 June 1865.

22 *Ibid.*, 20 April 1865.

23 Munby 33, 20 April 1865; Munby 34, 6 November 1866.

24 Munby 34, 25 October 1866.

25 Munby 36, 7 February 1868.

26 Munby 35, 5 and 21 February 1867.

27 Munby 18, p. 59.

28 Having said this, it should be pointed out that *flâneur* has become a highly contested term, open to a multiplicity of meanings way beyond that of the detached male observer; see D. Parsons, 'Flaneur or Flaneuse? Mythologies of Modernity', *New Formations*, 38 (1999), pp. 91–100; G. Gilloch, '"The Return of the Flaneur": The Afterlife of an Allegory', *New Formations*, 38 (1999), pp. 101–9.

29 Munby 35, 9 July 1867.

30 *Ibid.*, 23 July 1867.

31 Munby 18, pp. 74–8.

32 Munby 34, 11 May 1866.

33 Munby 33, 14 July 1865.

34 *Ibid.*, 1 September 1865.

35 Munby 34, 23 August 1866.

36 Munby 36, 10 February 1868.

37 Munby 33, 1 August 1865.

38 *Ibid.*, 1 September 1865.

39 *Ibid.*

40 C. Metz, 'Photography and Fetish', in C. Squiers, ed., *The Critical Image: Essays on Contemporary Photography* (Seattle, 1990), pp. 155–64.

41 A. McClintock, *Imperial Leather: Race, Gender and Sexuality in the Colonial Context* (London, 1995), p. 128.

42 Munby 34, 8 March 1866.

43 Munby 33, 30 November 1865.

44 Munby 34, 25 June and 15 August 1866.

45 Munby 35, 21 February 1867.

46 *Ibid.*, 21 March 1867.

47 *Ibid.*, 24 May and 18 June 1867.

48 For a good description of the essential characteristics of horror, see N. Carroll,

The Philosophy of Horror or Paradoxes of the Heart (New York, 1990). (The quotes come from pp. 23, 43, 57.)

49 Munby 97, Book 2, 16 October 1865.

50 Munby 38, p. 7.

51 Munby 35, 18 June 1867.

52 See E. K. Sedgwick, 'The Character in the Veil: Imagery of the Surface in the Gothic Novel', in her *The Coherence of Gothic Conventions* (New York, 1980), chap. 4; L. Jordanova, *Sexual Visions* (London, 1989), chap. 5; E. Showalter, *Sexual Anarchy* (London, 1991), chap. 8; R. Stott, 'Rider Haggard's Black Widow', in her *The Fabrication of the Late-Victorian Femme Fatale* (London, 1992), chap. 4, esp. pp. 96–8.

53 M. Lewis, *The Monk* [1796] (Oxford, 1995).

54 Sedgwick, *Gothic Conventions*, p. 143.

55 *Ibid.*, p. 11.

56 Munby 35, 18 June 1867. 'Monk' Lewis was the name given to Matthew Lewis after the success of his novel *The Monk* (see above).

57 Quoted in Stott, 'Rider Haggard's Black Widow', p. 112 (my emphasis).

58 N. Etherington, ed., *The Annotated She* (Bloomington, 1991), p. 194. This is retrogressive evolution: Stott, 'Rider Haggard's Black Widow', pp. 114–15.

59 Etherington, *The Annotated She*, p. 294.

60 Stott, 'Rider Haggard's Black Widow'. See also B. Dijkstra, *Idols of Perversity: Fantasies of Feminine Evil in Fin-de-siècle Culture* (New York, 1986), pp. 166–7, 290–91.

61 See also A. Hodgson, 'Defining the Species: Apes, Savages and Humans in Scientific and Literary Writing of the 1860s', *Journal of Victorian Culture*, 4 (1999), pp. 228–51.

62 Munby 34, 4 December 1866.

63 Munby 35, 18 June 1867.

64 'Faces', *Household Words*, 16 September 1854.

65 For literature, see G. Tytler, *Physiognomy in the European Novel* (Princeton, 1982). The best account of the cultural implications of belief in physiognomy is M. Cowling, *The Artist as Anthropologist: The Representation of Type and Character in Victorian art* (Cambridge, 1989). See also L. Hartley, *Physiognomy and the Meaning of Expression in Nineteenth-century Culture* (Cambridge, 2001).

66 Cowling, *Artist as Anthropologist*, p. 12.

67 For this, see *ibid.*, esp. chaps 2, 4.

68 Quoted in *ibid.*, p. 128.

69 See *ibid.*, p. 61.

70 J. Simms, *Nature's Revelations of Character* (New York, 1879), p. 217.

71 *Ibid.*, p. 246.

72 *Notes on Noses* (London, 1857), pp. 8–11 (quote from p. 10). See also J. Barter, *How to Read the Face and Head* (London, 1896).

73 Cowling, *Artist as Anthropologist*, p. 349.

74 *Ibid.*, pp. 350–52.

75 Munby 35, 2 August 1867.

76 *Ibid.*, 17 September 1867.

77 For the one-sex model, see T. Laqueur, *Making Sex: Body and Gender from the Greeks to Freud* (Cambridge, MA, 1990).

78 *Notes on Noses*, p. 107.

79 *Ibid.*, p. 111.

80 *Ibid.*, p. 116.

81 *Ibid.*, pp. 111–14.

82 *Ibid.*, pp. 108–10.

83 R. Cooper, 'Victorian Discourses on Women and Beauty: The Alexander Walker Texts', *Gender and History*, 5 (1993), pp. 40, 42.

84 T. Woolnoth, *The Study of the Human Face* (London, 1865), pp. 23–4, 177–9.

85 Simms, *Nature's Revelations*, p. 223.

86 Munby 9, p. 212.

87 Munby 33, 1 September 1865.

88 C. Darwin, *The Expression of the Emotions in Man and Animals* (Chicago, 1974), p. 327.

89 S. L. Gilman, *Creating Beauty to Cure the Soul: Race and Psychology in the Shaping of Aesthetic Surgery* (Durham, NC, 1998); *idem, Making the Body Beautiful: A Cultural History of Aesthetic Surgery* (Princeton, 1999).

90 Gilman, *Making the Body Beautiful*, esp. chaps 2–4.

91 See Gilman, 'Phantom of the Opera's Nose'; *idem, Creating Beauty*, chap. 5; *idem, Making the Body Beautiful*, chap. 2. For the nineteenth-century cultural milieu, see C. Bernheimer, *Figures of Ill Repute: Representing Prostitution in Nineteenth-century France* (Durham, NC, 1997).

92 Gilman, 'Phantom of the Opera's Nose'.

93 See also S. Zizek, 'Grimaces of the Real, or When the Phallus Appears', *October*, 58 (1991), pp. 45–68.

94 Munby 17, p. 125.

95 Quoted in Gilman, *Making the Body Beautiful*, p. 51.

96 L. Forbes, *Diseases of the Nose* (London, 1889), pp. 103–11.

97 See the image in S. L. Gilman, *Sexuality: An Illustrated History* (New York, 1989), p. 205 (the caption is Gilman's). One is reminded of Henry Mayhew's metaphor for his survey of prostitution: '... the philanthropist must overcome his repugnance to the task, and draw back the veil that is thinly spread over the skeleton.' See P. Quennel, ed., *London's Underworld* (London, 1952), p. 95. Mayhew's survey was published in 1862.

98 A. Corbin, *Time, Desire and Horror: Towards a History of the Senses* (Cambridge, 1995), p. 121.

99 See, most recently, E. Bronfen, *Over Her Dead Body: Death, Femininity and the Aesthetic* (New York, 1992). The theme of female death is long established; Gilman has discovered some striking images from the Middle Ages: Gilman, *Sexuality*, pp. 72–3.

100 N. Auerbach, *Woman and the Demon: The Life of a Victorian Myth* (Cambridge, MA, 1982), p. 41; Dijkstra, *Idols of Perversity*, p. 58.

101 Jordanova, *Sexual Visions*, chap. 5; Gilman, *Sexuality*, p. 249.

102 G. Leroux, *The Phantom of the Opera* [1910] (London, 1987), pp. 114–15.

103 A term usually used in connection with film; see B. Creed, *The Monstrous-feminine: Film, Feminism, Psychoanalysis* (London, 1993).

104 *Ibid.*, pp. 8–11.

105 K. Hurley, *The Gothic Body: Sexuality, Materialism, and Degeneration at the Fin de Siècle* (Cambridge, 1996), pp. 3–5. For the importance of theories of degeneration in European literature and political thought during this period, see D. Pick, *Faces of Degeneration: A European Disorder, c. 1848–c. 1918* (Cambridge, 1989); W. Greenslade, *Degeneration, Culture and the Novel 1880–1940* (Cambridge, 1994).

106 The image is reproduced in M. Russo, *The Female Grotesque: Risk, Excess and Modernity* (London, 1994), p. 115.

107 J. Halberstam, *Skin Shows: Gothic Horror and the Technology of Monsters* (Durham, NC, 1995), esp. chap. 1 (quote from p. 21). See also Russo, *Female*

Grotesque; J. J. Cohen, ed., *Monster Theory: Reading Culture* (Minneapolis, 1996).

108 Munby 35, 5 February 1867.

109 Orlan, *This Is My Body … This Is My Software* (London, 1996), p. 91.

3 Venus in Dirt: Servitude and Mastery

1 A. Munby, *Ann Morgan's Love* (London, 1896), p. 1.

2 *Ibid.*, pp. 30–31.

3 *The Spectator*, 7 March 1896.

4 *Ibid.*

5 Munby, *Ann Morgan's Love*, p. 10.

6 *Ibid.*, pp. 27, 31.

7 *Ibid.*, p. 15.

8 [A.J. Munby], *Susan* (London, 1893), p. 49.

9 *Ibid.*, p. 39.

10 *Ibid.*, p. 40.

11 *Ibid.*, p. 46.

12 *Ibid.*, p. 44.

13 The diaries and letters of Arthur J. Munby (1828–1910) and Hannah Cullwick (1833–1909), Trinity College Library, Cambridge [hereafter referred to as Munby], vol. 42, p. 45.

14 Munby, *Ann Morgan's Love*, p. 62.

15 Munby 63, pp. 14, 18.

16 *The Athenaeum*, 9 September 1893.

17 Munby 84, pp. 254–5.

18 S. Wildman and J. Christian, *Edward Burne-Jones Victorian Artist Dreamer* (New York, 1998), pp. 216–21. See also C. Arscott, 'Venus as Dominatrix: Nineteenth-century Artists and Their Creations', in C. Arscott and K. Scott, eds, *Manifestations of Venus: Art and Sexuality* (Manchester, 2000), chap. 6.

19 Munby 81, p. 148.

20 Munby 79a, pp. 20–21.

21 Munby 70, p. 35.

22 Munby 82, pp. 284–5.

23 Munby 75, pp. 76–7.

24 Munby 79b, pp. 69–70.

25 Munby 16, p. 249.

26 Munby 19, pp. 140–42.

27 Munby 87, p. 41.

28 Munby 70, pp. 10–11.

29 Munby 1, p. 13 (pp. 11–12 are missing).

30 Munby 7, p. 105.

31 Munby 82, p. 305.

32 Munby 58, p. 17.

33 Munby 41, 1 January 1873.

34 Munby 4, pp. 158–9.

35 Munby 82, pp. 151–5.

36 Munby 59a, p. 88.

37 Munby 34, 21 April 1866.

38 Munby 85, p. 285.

39 Munby, *Susan* , pp. 21–2.

40 [A.J. Munby], *Dorothy* (London, 1880).

41 Munby 12, pp. 146–7.

42 *Ibid.*, pp. 123–30 (quotes from pp. 124, 129–30).

43 Munby 91, p. 3.

44 Munby 84, p. 243.

45 This imagery comes from Munby 82 (1892), 85 (1893) and 86 (1896–8), but I could have used any of his journals.

46 Munby 91, pp. 46, 162.

47 Munby 86, p. 123.

48 Munby 85, p. 93.

49 Munby 87, pp. 99–103.

50 *The Bodley Head Bernard Shaw Collected Plays with Their Prefaces* (London, 1972), vol. 4, pp. 734–5.

51 Munby 99/1.

52 Munby 99/9.

53 Munby 98/4 (1870)

54 Munby 98/2 (1864).

55 *Ibid.*

56 *Ibid.*

57 Munby 17, pp. 109–11.

58 Munby 44, p. 37.

59 Munby 80, p. 36.

60 Munby 84, pp. 235–6.

61 See Munby 99/10, 13.

62 Munby 82, p. 311.

63 Munby 80, p. 36.

64 Munby 99/1.

65 Munby 42, p. 44.

66 Munby 82, p. 131.

67 *Ibid.*, pp. 135–6.

68 Munby 64, p. 72; see also Munby 42, pp. 9, 19, 61, 65; Munby 63, p. 30; Munby 82, pp. 165–6.

69 Munby 82, p. 202.

70 *Ibid.*, pp. 17–18.

71 *Ibid.* See also Munby 23, pp. 180–89.

72 Munby 87, pp. 55–6.

73 Munby 79a, p. 63.

74 Munby 6, pp. 20–23. He later crossed out the word *slave*, substituting *servant*, and erased the word *chimney*. Hudson provides the revised version in his extract; I have reverted to the original: D. Hudson, *Munby, Man of Two Worlds: The Life and Diaries of Arthur J. Munby 1828–1910* (London, 1974), p. 70.

75 Munby 6, pp. 29–46.

76 Munby 99/22.

77 Munby 75, p. 49.

78 *Ibid.*, pp. 48–58.

79 Munby 83, pp. 56–7.

80 Munby 44, p. 54.

81 Munby 85, p. 22.

82 Munby 42, p. 76.

83 Munby 70, p. 14.

84 Munby 99/13.

85 Munby 99/14.

86 Munby 99/22.

87 Munby 99/45.

88 Munby 99/46. The reference to 'ann' is presumably to Munby's *Ann Morgan's*

Love. The poem was not published until 1896, but it was obviously in manuscript before then – and Hannah had either read or heard it.

89 Munby 70, p. 15.

90 For example, *ibid.*, p. 18.

91 Munby 14, pp. 171–3.

92 *Ibid.*, pp. 187–9.

93 Munby 20, pp. 41–3.

94 For example, Munby 45, pp. 3, 5, 12, 13, 20, 27 (quote from p. 20).

95 See Munby 42, p. 6.

96 *Ibid.*

97 *Ibid.*, p. 76.

98 Munby 82, pp. 129–30, 141–3.

99 J. Ruskin, *Sesame and Lilies* (London, 1970), p. 48.

100 Munby, *Ann Morgan's Love*, p. 52.

101 Munby 85, p. 75.

102 Munby 77, p. 56.

103 Munby 19, pp. 226–7.

104 Munby 63, p. 168.

105 Munby 81, pp. 71–2, 92, 164.

106 Munby 86, pp. 38–9. See also his description of her reading of *David Copperfield*, acting out the characters with 'high dramatic power' in contrast to her lowly, rustic appearance: Munby 63, p. 156.

107 Munby 87, p. 134.

108 Munby 63, p. 22.

109 Munby 81, p. 110.

110 Munby 41, 7 May 1873.

111 Munby 86, pp. 126–7.

112 *Ibid.*, pp. 126–7, 132–3.

113 Munby 83, p. 56.

114 T. Hardy, *The Hand of Ethelberta: A Comedy in Chapters* [1876] (London, 1975).

115 The quotes from the novel come from F. H. Burnett, *That Lass O' Lowrie's: A Lancashire Story* [1877] (Bury St Edmunds, 1985), pp. 1, 3, 19, 103, 206.

116 Munby 84, pp. 191, 214, 233, 241, 257, 276–7, 318 (quote from p. 318).

117 For example, see Munby 34, 13 December 1866; Munby 35 (1867), *passim*.

118 [Anne Thackeray], 'The Village on the Cliff', *Cornhill Magazine*, 14 (July–December 1866), p. 3. Munby's diary for 2 December 1866 refers to a note that he wrote to Thackeray telling her that he too knew that women '*can* be "both gentle & strong"': Munby 34, 2 December 1866.

119 Thackeray, 'Village on the Cliff', pp. 488–9.

120 *Ibid.*, p. 9.

121 *Ibid.*, pp. 22–3.

122 *Ibid.*, pp. 148–9.

123 *Ibid.*, p. 512.

124 *Ibid.*, pp. 524–5.

125 *Ibid.*, pp. 526–7.

126 [Anne Thackeray], 'The Village on the Cliff', *Cornhill Magazine*, 15 (January–June 1867), p. 247. At first thought, it seems that it was a case of life imitating fiction. However, the interaction between fiction and life was not quite as clear-cut as it appears. Munby had confided to Thackeray about Cullwick at the time she was writing her story and thought the similarities too much of a coincidence, even though he had been told that Reine was based on a servant of the Thackerays (Hudson, *Munby*, p. 230; Munby 41, 24 October 1873).

127 Munby 75, p, 177.
128 'Queen Kara', in Jones Brown [A.J. Munby], *Vulgar Verses* (London, 1891),
    pp. 3–30.
129 [Munby], *Vulgar Verses*, p. 3:
    But this sad slave, could any call her fair,
    Through whose dark cheek no blush could ever rise,
    Nor her full lips the ruddy roses bear
    That take love's kiss ...
130 *Ibid.*, p. 11.
131 *Ibid.*, pp. 5, 23.
132 Munby 85, p. 259.
133 [Munby], *Vulgar Verses*, p. 28.
134 *Ibid.*, p. 29.
135 L. von Sacher-Masoch, 'Venus in Furs', in *Masochism* (New York, 1989),
    pp. 143–293.
136 Munby 86, p. 134.
137 Munby, *Susan*, p. 8.
138 Munby 109/1 (15).
139 Munby 91, pp. 92–3.
140 Munby 73, pp. 45–7; Munby 86, p. 128.
141 Munby 99/1.
142 Munby 99/23.
143 Munby 85, pp. 248–9.
144 Munby 79c, p. 39.
145 L. Stanley, ed., *The Diaries of Hannah Cullwick, Victorian Maidservant* (London,
    1984), p. 76.
146 Munby 75, pp. 58–69; see also Munby 66, pp. 31–4.
147 Munby 75, pp. 80–86; see also Munby 66, pp. 36, 54–60.
148 Munby 41, 2 May 1873.
149 *Ibid.*, 28 March 1873.
150 Munby 79c, pp. 9–11.
151 Munby 99/1.
152 Munby 4, pp. 128–30.
153 Munby 98/2.
154 Munby 14, p. 158.
155 Munby 84, p. 10.
156 See p. 71 above.
157 Munby, *Ann Morgan's Love*, p. 52.
158 See P. Gay, *The Bourgeois Experience, Victoria to Freud*: vol. 1: *Education of the
    Senses* (Oxford, 1984), pls betw. pp. 342 and 343.
159 G. Marshall, *Actresses on the Victorian Stage: Feminine Performance and the
    Galatea Myth* (Cambridge, 1998), esp. pp. 23, 113. This is just a starting point for
    a large literature.
160 D. Cherry and G. Pollock, 'Woman as Sign in Pre-Raphaelite Literature: A
    Study of the Representation of Elizabeth Siddall', *Art History*, 7 (1984),
    pp. 206–27 (quote from p. 216). See also J. Marsh, 'Imagining Elizabeth Siddal',
    History Workshop, 25 (1988), pp. 64–82; M. A. Danahay, 'Mirrors of Masculine
    Desire: Narcissus and Pygmalion in Victorian Representation', *Victorian Poetry*,
    32 (1994), pp. 35–53.
161 Hudson, *Munby*, p. 127. Danahay, 'Mirrors of Masculine Desire', pp. 45–6,
    makes the connection between Dante Gabriel Rossetti's Galateas and Munby's
    Cullwick.

162 V. Lee, *Miss Brown* (London, 1884), 3 vols; Garland Reprint 1978, vol. 1, pp. 118, 121–2.

163 *Ibid.*, vols 1, pp. 6, 15, 24–5, 50; 2, pp. 240, 307.

164 *Ibid.*, vol. 1, pp. 26, 51, 104–5, 222, 226, 304.

165 *Ibid.*, vol. 3, p. 48.

166 H. Fraser, 'Women and the Ends of Art History: Vision and Corporeality in Nineteenth-century Critical Discourse', *Victorian Studies*, 42 (1998/9), pp. 77–100 (quote from p. 88).

167 Lee, *Miss Brown*, vol. 1, p. 309 (quoted in Fraser, 'Women and the Ends of Art History', p. 88).

168 For a reading of *Miss Brown* as a lesbian text, see K. Psomiades, '"Still Burning from this Strangling Embrace": Vernon Lee on Desire and Aesthetics', in R. Dellamora, ed., *Victorian Sexual Dissidence* (Chicago, 1999), chap. 1.

4 Disordering Bodies: Gender Hybridity

1 The diaries and letters of Arthur J. Munby (1828–1910) and Hannah Cullwick (1833–1909), Trinity College Library, Cambridge [hereafter referred to as Munby], vol. 39, p. 77.

2 Munby 18, pp. 258–64.

3 Munby 37, 24 June 1869.

4 Munby 19, p. 86.

5 Munby 18, pp. 258–64.

6 Once a working woman had had her photograph taken, her image could be displayed in the shop window and copies ordered by anyone who cared to spend the money. See M. Hiley, *Victorian Working Women: Portraits from Life* (London, 1979), pp. 61–80.

7 Munby 40, pp. 12–13.

8 *Ibid.*, p. 81.

9 J. Butler, *Gender Trouble: Feminism and the Subversion of Identity* (New York, 1990), pp. 6–7, 17, 25, 139.

10 *Ibid.*, p. 112.

11 *Ibid.*, p. 127.

12 For just some examples, see J. L. Reich, 'Genderfuck: The Law of the Dildo', *Discourse*, 15 (1992), pp. 112–27; L. Doan, 'Jeanette Winterson's Sexing the Postmodern', in *idem*, *The Lesbian Postmodern* (New York, 1992), chap. 8; J. Halberstam, 'F2M: The Making of Female Masculinity', in Doan, ed., *Lesbian Postmodern*, chap. 12; R. Felski, 'Fin de Siècle, Fin de Sexe: Transexuality, Postmodernism, and the Death of History', *New Literary History*, 27 (1996), pp. 337–49; N. Hubbs, 'Music of the "Fourth Gender": Morrissey and the Sexual Politics of Melodic Contour', *Genders*, 23 (1996), pp. 266–96; C. Straayer, 'Postscript: A Graphic Interrogatory – Beyond Dimorphic Sex', in her *Deviant Eyes, Deviant Bodies: Sexual Re-orientations in Film and Video* (New York, 1996), pp. 253–87; S. Whittle, 'Gender Fucking or Fucking Gender?', in R. Elkins and D. King, eds, *Blending Genders: Social Aspects of Cross-dressing and Sex-changing* (London, 1996), chap. 14; R. Elkins, *Male Femaling: A Grounded Theory Approach to Cross-dressing and Sex-changing* (London, 1997); C. Jacob Hale, 'Leatherdyke Boys and Their Daddies: How to Have Sex without Women or Men', *Social Text*, 52/53 (1997), pp. 223–36; R. Elkins and D. King, 'Towards a Sociology of Transgendered Bodies', *Sociological Review*, 47 (1999), pp. 580–602; K. Shaffer, 'The Game Girls of VNS Matrix: Challenging Gendered Identities in Cyberspace', in M. A. O'Farrell and L. Vallone, eds, *Virtual Gender: Fantasies of Subjectivity and Embodiment* (Ann Arbor, 1999), pp. 147–68.

13 A. McClintock, *Imperial Leather: Race, Gender and Sexuality in the Colonial Context* (London, 1995), p. 101.

14 Munby 110/13: 'Female Labour: collection of newspaper cuttings by A.J. Munby'.

15 Munby 34, 18 February 1866.

16 Munby 35, 20 February 1867.

17 He also recorded a case from the *Medical Times* of a man who had passed as a woman for many years. He/she had worked as a cook until discovered by her employer: 'My dear creature, you are *a man*!' The employer had exhibited her to raise money to set her up as a man. Her hair had been cut short and (s)he had left in men's clothes to begin again as a dairyman. Munby noted that the woman had kept company with a man for six years '& *been forced* by him: and all that time she herself was a man': Munby 33, 3 December 1865.

18 Munby 4, pp. 43–4.

19 Munby 12, p. 237.

20 Munby 4, pp. 102–7.

21 Munby 12, pp. 222, 225.

22 Munby 24, p. 8.

23 [A. J. Munby], *Susan* (London, 1893), p. 8.

24 The term is Davidoff's: L. Davidoff, 'Class and Gender in Victorian England', in J. L. Newton, M. P. Ryan and J. R. Walkowitz, eds, *Sex and Class in Women's History* (London, 1983), p. 48.

25 Munby 39, pp. 51, 55.

26 Munby 16, pp. 88–119.

27 *Ibid.*, pp. 119–31.

28 For example, Munby 39, pp. 21, 24, 27, 32, 33.

29 Munby 37, 30 December 1869.

30 Munby 9, pp. 250–57.

31 Munby 109/11 (4): 'Elizabeth Shepstone'.

32 Munby 36, 7 September 1868.

33 Munby 39, 15 November 1871.

34 Munby 47, p. 16.

35 Munby 33, 25 April 1865.

36 Munby 39, p. 17.

37 Munby 33, 25 April 1865.

38 Munby 45, p. 16.

39 Munby 13, pp. 115–28. See also pp. 195–201.

40 Munby 25, pp. 178–82.

41 T. C. Davis, *Actresses as Working Women: Their Social Identity in Victorian Culture* (London, 1991), p. 15.

42 *The Stage*, 23 February 1893, quoted in Davis, *Actresses*, pp. 15–16.

43 Munby 17, p. 101.

44 *Ibid.*, pp. 99–103.

45 Munby 97, Book 7, pp. 61–2.

46 See Munby 97, Book 1, *passim*.

47 Munby 41, p. 10; G. Pollock, '"With My Own Eyes": Fetishism, the Labouring Body and the Colour of Its Sex', *Art History*, 17 (1994), pp. 367–8.

48 Munby 97, Book 4.

49 Munby 41, p. 84.

50 Munby 97, Book 1.

51 *Ibid.*

52 *Ibid.*

53 Munby 97, Book 3, p. 88.
54 For locals, of course, the male attire would have meant little; '… in Wigan, a woman in trousers is not half so odd as a woman in crinoline' (Munby 6, p. 205).
55 Munby 97, Book 1.
56 Munby 6, pp. 196–9.
57 The photographer was a woman, although the image is attributed to her husband, Robert Little, in Pollock's article.
58 Munby 41, p. 14. Pollock misses this part of Munby's description: Pollock, 'With My Own Eyes', pp. 369–71.
59 Munby 3, p. 24.
60 Pollock, 'With My Own Eyes', p. 371.
61 J. Plummer, 'A Real Social Evil', *Once a Week*, 27 August 1864.
62 Munby 39, p. 54.
63 Munby 11, pp. 249–53.
64 Munby 18, pp. 191–5; Munby 25, pp. 191–2.
65 Munby 97, Book 1.
66 McClintock, *Imperial Leather*, pp. 106–7.
67 Pollock, 'With My Own Eyes', pp. 344–6, 373–5. See also G. Pollock, 'The Dangers of Proximity: The Spaces of Sexuality and Surveillance in Word and Image', *Discourse*, 16 (1993–4), pp. 3–50.
68 See Munby 97, Book 3, p. 40; Book 8, pp. 15b, 34b, 47b.
69 Munby 97, Book 8, p. 44b.
70 Both Pollock and McClintock missed the complexity of the written descriptions, because they seem to have relied on transcripts of the Munby diaries rather than the original archives. Thus they have the sketch of Hayes, but not the diary description of her appearance.
71 Munby 97, Book 4.
72 Munby 41, p. 11.
73 Munby 97, Book 4.
74 *Ibid.*
75 Munby 41, p. 80.
76 Munby 97, Book 3, title page, pp. 18–20.
77 F. H. Burnett, *That Lass O' Lowrie's: A Lancashire Story* [1877] (Bury St Edmunds, 1985), pp. 1, 103.
78 C. Townsend, '"I Am the Woman for Spirit": A Working Woman's Gender Transgression in Victorian London', *Victorian Studies*, 36 (1993), pp. 293–314.
79 For late Victorian/Edwardian music-hall cross-dressing, see J. S. Bratton, 'Beating the Bounds: Gender Play and Role Reversal in the Edwardian Music Hall', in M. R. Booth and J. H. Kaplan, eds, *The Edwardian Theatre* (Cambridge, 1996), chap. 4.
80 Munby 4, pp. 6–7.
81 *Ibid.*, p. 136.
82 Munby 5, pp. 250–51.
83 Munby 39, p. 17. But for an article by Laurence Senelick, which refers to Lulu's androgyny, this historian would have been tricked too: L. Senelick, 'Boys and Girls Together: Subcultural Origins of Glamour Drag and Male Impersonation on the Nineteenth-century Stage', in L. Ferris, ed., *Crossing the Stage: Controversies on Cross-dressing* (London, 1993), p. 84. See also S. Peacock, 'Farini the Great', *Bandwagon* (September–October 1990), pp. 13–20.
84 For example, Greta Garbo in *Queen Christina* (1933); Cary Grant in *I Was a Male War Bride* (1949); Tony Curtis and Jack Lemmon in *Some Like It Hot* (1959); Julie Andrews in *Victor/Victoria* (1982); Dustin Hoffman in *Tootsie* (1982); and

Barbara Streisand in *Yentl* (1983). See C. Straayer, 'Redressing the "Natural": The Temporary Transvestite Film', in B. K. Grant, ed., *Film Genre Reader II* (Austin, 1992), chap. 25.

85 *Ibid.*, p. 407.

86 M. Garber, *Vested Interests: Cross-dressing and Cultural Anxiety* (New York, 1997), pp. 9–10, 17, 147, 150.

87 Severo Sarduy, quoted in Garber, *Vested Interests*, p. 150.

88 J. Halberstam, *Female Masculinity* (Durham, NC, 1998), pp. 276–7. See also D. Lagrace Volcano and J. 'Jack' Halberstam, *The Drag King Book* (London, 1999).

89 When I use the word *heterosexual*, I am referring to 'heterosexuality' before heterosexuality.

90 Munby 41, pp. 5, 8.

91 Munby 110/18 (4).

92 Munby 17, p. 145.

93 Munby 14, pp. 106–8.

94 Munby 80, pp. 41–2.

5 Dorothy's Hands: Feminizing Men

1 The diaries and letters of Arthur J. Munby (1828–1910) and Hannah Cullwick (1833–1909), Trinity College Library, Cambridge [hereafter referred to as Munby], vol. 14, p. 140.

2 Munby 5, pp. 226–8.

3 J. K. Huysmans, *Against the Grain (À Rebours)* [1884] (New York, 1969), pp. 98–9.

4 Munby 6, pp. 30, 34.

5 Munby 9, pp. 250–57.

6 A. Munby, *Ann Morgan's Love* (London, 1896), p. 10.

7 Munby 7, pp. 80–82.

8 *Ibid.*, p. 83.

9 Munby 59, p. 109a

10 D. Hudson, *Munby, Man of Two Worlds: The Life and Diaries of Arthur J. Munby 1828–1910* (London, 1974), p. 31.

11 Munby 4, pp. 121–2.

12 Munby 12, pp. 1–5.

13 Munby 24, pp. 2–3.

14 Munby 91, pp. 92–3. And see Chapter 3 above.

15 J. Simms, *Nature's Revelations of Character* (New York, 1879), pp. 390–95.

16 M. Cowling, *The Artist as Anthropologist: The Representation of Type and Character in Victorian Art* (Cambridge, 1989), p. 349.

17 R. Beamish, *Psychonomy of the Hand* (London, 1865), pls 1, 3.

18 Munby 109/11 (4): 'Elizabeth Shepstone'.

19 Munby 9, pp. 250–57.

20 Munby 109/11 (4): 'Elizabeth Shepstone'.

21 T. Hardy, *The Hand of Ethelberta: A Comedy in Chapters* [1876] (London, 1975), p. 366. As discussed in Chapter 3, this novel was a favourite with Munby and Cullwick.

22 Beamish, *Psychonomy of the Hand*, p. 85.

23 W. A. Cohen, *Sex Scandal: The Private Parts of Victorian Fiction* (Durham, NC, 1996), p. 35.

24 *Ibid.*, chap. 2: 'Manual Conduct in *Great Expectations*' (quote from p. 34).

25 Carol Mavor, *Pleasures Taken: Performances of Sexuality and Loss in Victorian Photographs* (Durham, NC, 1995), p. 92.

26 *Seinfeld*, Episode 66: 'The Puffy Shirt', first broadcast on 23 September 1993.

27 *Ibid.*

28 Oscar Wilde, *The Picture of Dorian Gray* [first published in book form 1891] (Ware, 1992) [Wordsworth Classic edition, intro Joseph Bristow], pp. 22–3, 37, 62, 63, 70–71, 72.

29 *Ibid.*, pp. 31–2, 98, 103, 138, 176.

30 *Ibid.*, pp. 20, 130, 139, 142, 146, 168–9.

31 E. Cohen, *Talk on the Wilde Side: Toward a Genealogy of Discourse on Male Sexualities* (New York, 1993), pp. 139–42; A. Sinfield, *The Wilde Century: Effeminacy, Oscar Wilde and the Queer Moment* (London, 1994), p. 2; J. Bristow, 'Wilde's Fatal Effeminacy', in his *Effeminate England: Homoerotic Writing after 1885* (Buckingham, 1995), pp. 31, 33.

32 Sinfield, *Wilde Century*, p. 73.

33 Cohen, *Talk on the Wilde Side*, p. 136. See also Bristow, *Effeminate England*, p. 42.

34 T. Castle, *Noël Coward and Radclyffe Hall: Kindred Spirits* (New York, 1996), pp. 40, 42.

35 G. W. Henry, *Sex Variants: A Study of Homosexual Patterns* (New York, 1941) [a study sponsored by the Committee for the Study of Sex Variants], pp. 62, 64, 117, 119, 231, 242, 283, 291, 314, 342, 350, 370.

36 *Ibid.*, pp. 611, 613, 626, 711, 739, 741, 761, 776, 818, 820, 830, 867, 972, 1009.

37 M. Merck, 'The Lesbian Hand', in her *In Your Face: 9 Sexual Studies* (New York, 2000), chap. 7 (quote from p. 127).

38 *The Memoirs of John Addington Symonds*, ed. P. Grosskurth (London, 1984), p. 65.

39 *Ibid.*, pp. 82, 97–8.

40 *Ibid.*, pp. 104–5, 183.

41 *Ibid.*, p. 190.

42 *Ibid.*, p. 210.

43 H. Ellis, *Studies in the Psychology of Sex* (London, 1948), vol. 1, p. 142 (my italics). See also *Memoirs of John Addington Symonds*, p. 287.

44 [A.J. Munby], *Dorothy* (London, 1880), pp. 20, 45, 48.

45 C. Craft, *Another Kind of Love: Male Homosexual Desire in English Discourse, 1850–1920* (Berkeley, 1994), chap. 3.

46 *Ibid.*, p. 75.

47 Munby, *Dorothy*, p. 20.

48 I. de Courtivron, 'Weak Men and Fatal Women: The Sand Image', in G. Stambolian and E. Marks, eds, *Homosexualities and French Literature: Cultural Contexts / Critical Texts* (Ithaca, NY, 1979), pp. 210–27.

49 T. E. Morgan, 'Male Lesbian Bodies: The Construction of Alternative Masculinities in Courbet, Baudelaire, and Swinburne', *Genders*, 15 (1992), pp. 37–57 (quotes from pp. 40, 46).

50 Hudson, *Munby*, p. 283 (emphasis in original).

51 Munby 34, p. 24 (partially quoted in Hudson, *Munby*, p. 220).

52 R. Dellamora, *Masculine Desire: The Sexual Politics of Victorian Aestheticism* (Chapel Hill, 1990), pp. 1–2, 218.

53 Hudson, *Munby*, pp. 403–4 (emphasis in original).

6 Sexuating Arthur

1 The 'sexuating' in the title of this chapter comes from Carol Mavor, *Pleasures Taken: Performances of Sexuality and Loss in Victorian Photographs* (Durham, NC, 1995), p. 84, where she discusses the sexuality of Hannah Cullwick.

2 R. von Krafft-Ebing, *Psychopathia Sexualis* [1886] (New York, 1998), pp. 173–4.

3 S. Marcus, *The Other Victorians: A Study of Sexuality and Pornography in Mid-nineteenth Century England* (London, 1966), chaps 3–4.

4 *Ibid.*, pp. 88, 95, 188, 193.

5 *Ibid.*, p. 185.

6 For the latest intervention on the nature and authorship of *My Secret Life*, see I. Gibson, *The Erotomaniac: The Secret Life of Henry Spencer Ashbee* (London, 2001). Gibson is less than convincing in his attribution of authorship to Ashbee, but if he were correct, the comparison with Munby would be still more intriguing because Gibson sees the whole work as a 'fictional substitute' for an unattainable sexual life (p. 231).

7 The diaries and letters of Arthur J. Munby (1828–1910) and Hannah Cullwick (1833–1909), Trinity College Library, Cambridge [hereafter referred to as Munby], vol. 25, pp. 164–8.

8 Munby 8, p. 204.

9 Munby 1, pp. 14–19.

10 Munby 12, pp. 56–7.

11 Munby 25, pp. 126–7.

12 J. Walkowitz, *City of Dreadful Delight: Narratives of Sexual Danger in Late-Victorian London* (London, 1992).

13 Munby 25, pp. 136–7.

14 Munby 12, pp. 220–29.

15 Munby 13, pp. 128–31.

16 Munby 33, 22 April 1865.

17 Munby 34, 1 August 1866.

18 *Ibid.*

19 D. E. Nord, *Walking the Victorian Streets: Women, Representation, and the City* (Ithaca, NY, 1995), pp. 42–6.

20 Munby 24, pp. 86–9. Munby was taken aback by the offer and did not think it typical practice. For minstrelsy, see M. Pickering, 'White Skins, Black Masks: "Nigger" Minstrelsy in Victorian Britain', in J. S. Bratton, ed., *Music Hall: Performance and Style* (Milton Keynes, 1986), pp. 78–90; E. Lott, *Love and Theft: Blackface Minstrelsy and the American Working Class* (New York, 1995).

21 Munby 38, pp. 53, 57–8. For a discussion of the role of the actress's body in Victorian pornography, applicable to female acrobats, see T. C. Davis, 'The Actress in Victorian Pornography', in K. O. Garrigan, ed., *Victorian Scandals: Representations of Gender and Class* (Athens, OH, 1992), chap. 4.

22 Munby 39, 11 May 1871. See also Munby 34, 21 April 1866.

23 For a critical introduction to the opera, see P. Robinson, *Ludwig van Beethoven: Fidelio* (Cambridge, 1996).

24 See the illustration in *ibid.*, p. 151.

25 *Ibid.*, p. 97.

26 Munby 75, pp. 98–100.

27 Robinson, *Fidelio*, pp. 96–7.

28 Munby 42, p. 46.

29 Munby 44, p. 43.

30 See Munby 82, p. 311; Munby 98/2.

31 Munby 6, p. 22.

32 *Ibid.*, pp. 61–2.

33 Munby 14, p. 174.

34 Munby 99/1.

35 Munby 40, p. 48.

36 Munby 84, p. 170.

37 Munby 81, p. 149. See L. Stanley, ed., *The Diaries of Hannah Cullwick, Victorian Maidservant* (London, 1984), p. 14 ('Their relationship was almost certainly never sexual in any conventional and genital sense before marriage, perhaps not after it either'); L. Davidoff, 'Class and Gender in Victorian England', in J. L. Newton, M. P. Ryan and J. R. Walkowitz, eds, *Sex and Class in Women's History* (London, 1983), p. 38 ('… there are some indications that Munby may have been impotent').

38 C. Parker, 'Gender Roles and Sexuality in R. D. Blackmore's Other Novels', in C. Parker, ed., *Gender Roles and Sexuality in Victorian Literature* (Aldershot, 1995), chap. 4. Munby's poetic tribute to Blackmore actually refers to his 'manly self-control': D. Hudson, *Munby, Man of Two Worlds: The Life and Diaries of Arthur J. Munby 1828–1910* (London, 1974), p. 425.

39 Munby 81, p. 67.

40 J. M. Lloyd, 'Conflicting Expectations in Nineteenth-century British Matrimony: The Failed Companionate Marriage of Effie Gray and John Ruskin', *Journal of Women's History*, 11 (1999), pp. 86–109. See also T. Hilton, *John Ruskin: The Early Years* (New Haven, 1985), pp. 117–20.

41 Munby 85, p. 60.

42 Munby 99/22.

43 Munby 87, p. 44.

44 Munby 83, pp. 86–7.

45 Munby 87, p. 56.

46 *Ibid.*

47 Munby 80, pp. 35–6, 41–2.

48 Munby 81, p. 67.

49 Munby 80, pp. 92–3.

50 Munby 79c, p. 63.

51 Munby 74, pp. 76–7, 84–5.

52 Munby 99/33(2).

53 Munby 75, pp. 117–21. See also Munby 17, pp. 148–50.

54 E. McEvoy, 'Introduction' to M. Lewis, *The Monk* (Oxford, 1995), pp. xxiv, xxvi. The quote comes from p. 243 of this edition of the novel, where the falling Monk compares the virgin and the 'wanton': 'Oh! sweeter must one kiss be snatched from the rosy lips of the First, than all the full and lustful favours bestowed so freely by the Second.' Munby had read *The Monk*; see Chapter 2.

55 M. Homans, 'Dinah's Blush, Maggie's Arm: Class, Gender, and Sexuality in George Eliot's Early novels', *Victorian Studies*, 36 (1993), pp. 155–78 (reprint in A. H. Miller and J. E. Adams, eds, *Sexualities in Victorian Britain* [Bloomington, 1996], chap. 2).

56 Munby 35, 15 July 1867.

57 V. Rosario, *The Erotic Imagination: French Histories of Perversity* (New York, 1997), p. 129.

58 J. K. Noyes, *The Mastery of Submission: Inventions of Masochism* (Ithaca, NY, 1997), p. 4.

59 Z. Bauman, 'Desert Spectacular', in K. Tester, ed., *The Flaneur* (London, 1994), pp. 142, 145, 146.

60 See p. 35 above.

61 See R. Nye, 'The Medical Origins of Sexual Fetishism', in E. Apter and W. Pietz, eds, *Fetishism as Cultural Discourse* (Ithaca, NY, 1993), pp. 13–30; Rosario, *Erotic Imagination*, chap. 4: 'Fetishists: Cults, Consumption, and Erotic Dramas'.

62 Rosario, *Erotic Imagination*, pp. 114, 126.

63 D. Ades, 'Surrealism: Fetishism's Job', in A. Shelton, ed., *Fetishism: Visualising*

Power and Desire (London, 1995), pp. 67–87 (quote from p. 73).

64 Davidoff, 'Class and Gender'; P. Stallybrass and A. White, *The Politics and Poetics of Transgression* (Ithaca, NY, 1986), chap. 4: 'Below Stairs: The Maid and the Family Romance'; E. Apter, *Feminizing the Fetish: Psychoanalysis and Narrative Obsession in Turn-of-the-century France* (Ithaca, NY, 1991), chap. 8: 'Master Narratives/Servant Texts: Representing the Maid from Flaubert to Freud'; A. Corbin, 'The Archaeology of the Housewife and Bourgeois Fantasies', in his *Time, Desire and Horror: Towards a History of the Senses* (Cambridge, 1995), chap. 4 (quote from p. 64).

65 Apter, *Feminizing the Fetish*, p. 178.

66 Stallybrass and White, *Politics and Poetics of Transgression*, p. 154.

67 A. McClintock, *Imperial Leather: Race, Gender and Sexuality in the Colonial Context* (New York, 1995), p. 142.

68 M. Mason, *The Making of Victorian Sexual Attitudes* (Oxford, 1994).

69 S. Szreter, *Fertility, Class and Gender in Britain, 1860–1940* (Cambridge, 1996), chap. 8: 'How was Fertility Controlled? The Spacing Versus Stopping Debate and the Culture of Abstinence'. For a fruitful interaction between the ideas of Mason and Szreter, see S. Szreter, 'Victorian Britain, 1831–1963: Towards a Social History of Sexuality', *Journal of Victorian Culture*, 1 (1996), pp. 136–49, and Mason's review of Szreter's book and Szreter's reply in the Institute of Historical Research's web-based journal, *Reviews in History*, Review No. 5.

70 W. Graham, *Henry James's Thwarted Love* (Stanford, 1999), chap. 1, esp. pp. 11–12.

71 *Ibid.*, pp. 26–7.

72 *Ibid.*, p. 28.

73 A. J. L. Busst, 'The Image of the Androgyne in the Nineteenth Century', in I. Fletcher, ed., *Romantic Mythologies* (London, 1967), p. 43.

74 McClintock, *Imperial Leather*, p.78.

75 This curiously neglected but important piece was the first serious attempt to move beyond the debate about repression versus permissiveness in Victorian sexuality: S. Seidman, 'The Power of Desire and the Danger of Pleasure: Victorian Sexuality Reconsidered', *Journal of Social History*, 24 (1990), pp. 47–67. See also J. Maynard, *Victorian Discourses on Sexuality and Religion* (Cambridge, 1993).

76 It is interesting to compare a later, more obvious case of personal panic. The British film director Lindsay Anderson combined (homosexual) celibacy with crushes on unavailable (heterosexual) male actors. See the recent semi-biography, G. Lambert, *Mainly about Lindsay Anderson – A Memoir* (London, 2000).

77 E. K. Sedgwick, *Epistemology of the Closet* (Berkeley and Los Angeles, 1990), chap. 4: 'The Beast in the Closet: James and the Writing of Homosexual Panic'.

78 Graham, *Henry James's Thwarted Love*, chap. 1.

79 For the bachelor in America, see H. P. Chudacoff, *The Age of the Bachelor: Creating an American Subculture* (Princeton, 1999). It could be argued that John Tosh's recent account of middle-class masculinity neglects the role of the bachelor in Victorian English culture (*A Man's Place: Masculinity and the Middle-class Home in Victorian England* [New Haven, 1999]).

80 H. Sussman, *Victorian Masculinities: Manhood and Masculine Poetics in Early Victorian Literature and Art* (Cambridge, 1995), chap. 3.

81 Miller and Adams, 'Introduction' in Miller and Adams, eds, *Sexualities*, p. 7.

82 A. Frazier, *George Moore, 1852–1933* (New Haven and London, 2000), p. 424.

83 G. Moore, *Celibates* (London, 1895), pp. 146, 247.

84 Hilton, *John Ruskin: The Early Years*, pp. 117–20.

85 Frazier, *George Moore*, p. 150.

86 Moore, *Celibates*, pp. 332, 336, 344, 345, 441.

87 *Ibid.*, pp. 369, 394–6.

88 G. Moore, *Celibate Lives* (London, 1927), pp. 44–96.

89 See Frazier, *George Moore*, index under 'homosexuality'.

90 Frazier, *George Moore*, p. 247.

91 *Ibid.*, pp. 182–3.

92 A. Frazier, 'On His Honor: George Moore and Some Women', *English Literature in Transition 1880–1920*, 35 (1992), p. 428.

93 P. Bailey, 'Parasexuality and Glamour: The Victorian Barmaid as Cultural Prototype', *Gender and History*, 2 (1990), pp. 148–72 (reprint as chap. 7 in his *Popular Culture and Performance in the Victorian City* [Cambridge, 1998]).

94 Normally used in relation to the football pools: see *The Penguin Reference Dictionary* (Harmondsworth, 1985).

95 For a promising recent discussion of Victorian polymorphous sex, rather more explicitly genitally focused than my account, see D. E. Hall, 'Graphic Sexuality and the Erasure of a Polymorphous Perversity', in D. E. Hall and M. Pramaggiore, eds, *RePresenting Bisexualities: Subjects and Cultures of Fluid Desire* (New York, 1996), chap. 4. And for a suggestive discussion of dispersed sexuality, with elements of both agency and objectification comparable to Munby's stagings, see E. B. Rosenman, 'Spectacular Women: *The Mysteries of London* and the Female Body', *Victorian Studies*, 40 (1996), pp. 31–64.

Postscript

1 A. J. Munby, 'Pastrana', in his *Relicta* (London, 1909), pp. 5–13.

2 See J. Bondeson, 'Julia Pastrana, the Nondescript', *American Journal of Medical Genetics*, 47 (1993), pp. 198–212; J. Bondeson, *A Cabinet of Medical Curiosities* (Ithaca, NY, 1997), pp. 216–44.

3 The diaries and letters of Arthur J. Munby (1828–1910) and Hannah Cullwick (1833–1909), Trinity College Library, Cambridge [hereafter referred to as Munby], vol. 12, pp. 204–7.

4 Bondeson, *Cabinet*.

5 Munby 12, pp. 208–9.

6 Munby, 'Pastrana'.

7 See A. Callen, *The Spectacular Body: Science, Method and Meaning in the Work of Degas* (New Haven, 1995), chap. 1, esp. pp. 21–9 (quote from p. 28).

8 Munby 12, p. 210.

9 Munby 13, p. 192.

10 [A.J. Munby], *Dorothy* (London, 1880), pp. viii–xiii.

11 Munby 39, p. 63. For the comment by Sussman, see H. Sussman, *Victorian Masculinities: Manhood and Masculine Poetics in Early Victorian Literature and Art* (Cambridge, 1995), p. 141.

12 Most recently, J. Walkowitz, *City of Dreadful Delight: Narratives of Sexual Danger in Late-Victorian London* (London, 1992), p. 21. It was true also of twentieth-century documentary representation of the poor; see P. Rabinowitz, *They Must Be Represented: The Politics of Documentary* (London, 1994), esp. chap. 2, where she compares Munby to James Agee and Walker Evans's *Let Us Now Praise Famous Men*.

13 C. R. Forker, 'The Language of Hands in *Great Expectations*', *Texas Studies in Literature and Language*, 3 (1961), pp. 280–93; M. Hollington, 'Dickens the Flâneur', *Dickensian*, 77 (1981), pp. 71–87.

14 G. Marshall, *Actresses on the Victorian Stage: Feminine Performance and the Galatea Myth* (Cambridge, 1998), esp. chaps 1–2 (pp. 16–17 for the sexologists); C. Arscott, 'Venus as Dominatrix: Nineteenth-century Artists and Their Creations', in C. Arscott and K. Scott, eds, *Manifestations of Venus: Art and Sexuality* (Manchester, 2000), chap. 6. See also J. L. Carr, 'Pygmalion and the *Philosophes*: The Animated Statue in Eighteenth-century France', *Journal of the Warburg and Courtauld Institutes*, 23 (1960), p. 239, for the Enlightenment quote; and Havelock Ellis, *Studies in the Psychology of Sex* (London, 1948), vol. 1, p. 188, for the erotomania.

15 J. D. Reid, *The Oxford Guide to Classical Mythology in the Arts, 1300–1990s* (New York, 1993), vol. 2, pp. 955–62. See also C. Maxwell, 'Browning's Pygmalion and the Revenge of Galatea', *ELH*, 60 (1993), pp. 989–1013; M. A. Danahay, 'Mirrors of Masculine Desire: Narcissus and Pygmalion in Victorian Representation', *Victorian Poetry*, 32 (1994), pp. 35–53; S. Guy-Bray, 'Beddoes, Pygmalion, and the Art of Onanism', *Nineteenth-Century Literature*, 52 (1997–8), pp. 446–70.

16 L. Davidoff, 'Class and Gender in Victorian England', in J. L. Newton, M. P. Ryan and J. R. Walkowitz, eds, *Sex and Class in Women's History* (London, 1983), chap. 1; P. Stallybrass and A. White, *The Politics and Poetics of Transgression* (Ithaca, NY, 1986), chap. 4: 'Below Stairs: The Maid and the Family Romance'; E. Apter, *Feminizing the Fetish: Psychoanalysis and Narrative Obsession in Turn-of-the-century France* (Ithaca, NY, 1991), chap. 8: 'Master Narratives/Servant Texts: Representing the Maid from Flaubert to Freud'; A. Corbin, 'The Archaeology of the Housewife and Bourgeois Fantasies', in his *Time, Desire and Horror: Towards a History of the Senses* (Cambridge, 1995), chap. 4. The fantasy continues in some circles. The English writer Simon Raven, who died recently, was said to have recommended a massage parlour opposite the Reform Club, 'where you got "a good housemaid's wank"'. See the obituary in *Guardian Weekly*, 24–30 May 2001.

17 A. Solomon-Godeau, 'The Legs of the Countess', in E. Apter and W. Pietz, eds, *Fetishism as Cultural Discourse* (Ithaca, NY, 1993), pp. 266–306.

18 E. Lipton, *Looking into Degas: Uneasy Images of Women and Modern Life* (Berkeley and Los Angeles, 1986).

19 A. Frazier, *George Moore, 1852–1933* (New Haven and London, 2000), p. 138.

20 G. Pollock, '"With My Own Eyes": Fetishism, the Labouring Body and the Colour of Its Sex', *Art History*, 17 (1994), p. 348.

21 G. Pollock, 'The "View from Elsewhere": Extracts from a Semi-public Correspondence about the Politics of Feminist Spectatorship', in P. Florence and D. Reynolds, eds, *Feminist Subjects, Multi-media* (Manchester, 1995), chap. 1.

22 N. Ross, *Manet's Bar at the Folies-Bergère and the Myths of Popular Illustration* (Ann Arbor, 1982), p. 77.

23 T. Garb, *Bodies of Modernity: Figure and Flesh in Fin-de-siècle France* (London, 1998), chaps 1, 7.

24 T. J. Clark, 'Olympia's Choice', in his *The Painting of Modern Life: Paris in the Art of Manet and His Followers* (London, 1990), pp. 87, 92, 94, 96–7.

25 See also the important work by Charles Bernheimer, *Figures of Ill Repute: Representing Prostitution in Nineteenth-century France* (Durham, NC, 1997).

Acknowledgements

The author and publishers wish to express their thanks to the following sources of illustrative material and/or permission to reproduce it: Birmingham Museums and Art Gallery: 32; Courtauld Gallery, Courtauld Institute, London: 93; Dunedin Public Art Gallery, New Zealand: 1, 3; © photo RMN, Paris, the artist: 65; Musée d'Orsay, Paris: 94; National Gallery of Art, Washington, DC: 91; National Gallery of Australia, Canberra: title-page vignette; National Library of Medicine, Bethesda, MD: 31; © Tate, London: 2, 6, 27; Master and Fellows of Trinity College, Cambridge: 7–24, 33–6, 38–62, 66–85, 87–90, 92.

The author would particularly like to thank Li-Ming Hu for her assistance with checking quotations and references, and Eve Kosofsky Sedgwick for permission to use the quotation on the jacket.

Readers should note that the diaries and letters of Arthur Munby and Hannah Cullwick have been copied to microfilm (32 reels), and are commercially available as 'Working Women in Victorian Britain, 1850–1910' (Marlborough: Adam Matthew Publications, 1993). While this certainly makes for easier scholarly access, it is still necessary to consult the Trinity College originals when working with the sketches and photographs.

Index

Numbers in *italics* indicate pages with illustrations.